MEMORIES
MADE IN ASTON
A Book for the Fans written by the Fans

About the Author

Simon Goodyear (45) resides in Warwickshire and is a life long Aston Villa fan and is the son of the late author, historian and former employee of Aston Villa FC, David Goodyear. His first book *The Gerry Hitchens Story – From Mine to Milan* started as a labour of love in 2008 but it proved to be such a life changing experience and a success for Simon that he decided to continue his writing talents with the publication of *The Bobby Thomson Story – The Real Bobby Dazzler.*

MEMORIES
MADE IN ASTON
A Book for the Fans written by the Fans

Foreword by Ian Taylor

Compiled by Simon Goodyear

First published in Great Britain in 2011 by The Derby Books Publishing Company Limited, 3 The Parker Centre, Derby, DE21 4SZ

© **Simon Goodyear, 2011**

ISBN 978-1-85983-989-8

Printed and bound in Poland.
www.polskabook.co.uk

Contents

Foreword
by Ian Taylor

Ian Taylor is a lifelong Villa supporter and used to stand on the Holte End as a child. It is perhaps for this reason, combined with his truly committed displays and knack of scoring crucial goals, that he quickly became a fans' favourite. Ian was signed from Sheffield Wednesday for around £1m by Brian Little in December 1994 and made 290 appearances scoring 42 goals in all competitions before signing for Derby County in 2003.

Now retired from the game, Ian is still involved with his boyhood club as he was appointed the club ambassador in February 2011.

It is every Villa fans dream to pull on that claret and blue shirt; however, very few achieve it. There are a few in this book and I am totally honoured to be one of that few. It's hard, when asked to describe the feeling of walking out in front of a packed Villa Park and scoring in big games. But this is what dreams are made of. My home debut at Villa Park was against Chelsea on 28 December 1994, an evening match - always the best. The world and his dog of my family were there to see me. The obvious hairs on the back of my neck stood up as I walked out of that Trinity Road tunnel. To be walking out with most of the heroes of that famous League Cup win against Manchester United two years previously was enough; I was actually at as a spectator while playing for Port Vale at the time! But to score a goal in front of the legendary Holte End with my closest family and friends on the night was the absolute pinnacle. I've felt the good feelings of the Villa faithful ever since and giving a 100% everytime I put on that claret and blue shirt and hopefully it went a long way to paying back that faith.

Keep the faith,

Up the Villa!

Tayls

Preface
A Note From The Author

I must admit that the inspiration for this book was actually given to me by a Wolves fan and fellow author, Dave Instone (Thomas Publications), who incidentally had previously published the book called *Forever Villa*. With the seed sowed, the rest seemed to be a natural progression and the ideas for the book followed swiftly. Having written two books previously, I knew my publishers would be keen to take on this very unique, but fairly risky idea. And so they did.

The idea of compiling a book of mainly memories from the past is somewhat unique and certainly hasn't been done before as far as Aston Villa is concerned, let alone any other club that I am aware of, although I understand that the basic idea had been thought of before by several people but a final book had never been put into production. Initially, I thought a book consisting of dozens and dozens of memories written by fans would seem to be a bit monotonous so I included a number of other topics like Villa related poems, historical facts, favourite Villa kits from the past, a bit of trivia and some one-liners. Throw in a few original pictures relating to some of the stories and add to that recollections from a number of former Villa players and a few celebrities then you have got the recipe for an excellent book that you the fans would hopefully really appreciate.

My association with the Aston Villa Former Players Association made it possible for me to be allowed access to the former players and I think that their input was invaluable. It was a real privilege to talk to some of the '82 lads especially; the likes of Tony Morley, Gary Shaw and Ken McNaught to name but a few who provided me with some terrific stories from their times playing in that great side. Other great characters such as Jimmy Brown, the youngest player to put on a Villa shirt, the great Peter McParland and Chris Nicholl for me were also brilliant to listen to. Not only that, using my contacts with local journalists in placing articles in the Birmingham press asking the public to contact me with their stories helped enormously. So did scouring several internet based fans websites and letting all my Villa friends know about this project helped my pursuit of the vital stories that would take up a large chunk of this book. I had dozens and dozens of stories flooding into my inbox and fans from all over the world made contact to tell me their memories watching this great club. I had contacts from as far as Australia, France, The Philippines and Ireland. People of all ages, from 90-year-old ladies to people who wanted to recall more recent matches contacted me with great pleasure and enthusiasm. I also visited several people and interviewed them in their homes and listened to their great and interesting stories of times gone by.

The end result is this fascinating book, *Memories Made In Aston*, which I hope you will enjoy and maybe it will stir up some long lost memories of watching this great club we all love and support. Sit back and enjoy the trip back in time.

Simon Goodyear
www.soccerbiographies.com

Acknowledgements

Compiling and producing a book of this nature would always require input and help from many people. In the case of *Memories Made In Aston*, I was lucky enough to have been sent so many fantastic stories and pictures from Villa fans from all over the world and these make up the majority of the fans entries you will find in this book. Not only that, I also had the pleasure to interview a number of fans who spoke to me with both pride and passion about their recollections from times gone by. Of course, when you talk about fans, you can include the former players who also spoke of their times playing for Villa with pride, especially the '82 lads who quite rightly stand out as examples of players who reached the pinnacle of their playing career by winning football's biggest prize – The European Cup.

Furthermore, I am truly grateful to all the poets who have contributed to a superb cultural section of Villa based poems which I hope everyone will find appealing, even if you are not into football verse. At worst it was meant to be a bit of light hearted fun.

I would also like to thank Neil Rioch and the Aston Villa Former Players' Association who have backed this project and allowed me permission to interview the former players who have contributed to the book and I am pleased to say that half of the proceeds from the book will be donated to AVFPA. Furthermore, I would like to show my appreciation to one of my favourite players, Ian Taylor who has contributed to a superb forward. Thank you Tayls.

Further acknowledgements include Danny Drewry from Midlands Memorabilia, Mat Kendrick of the *Birmingham Mail*, Martin Swain of the *Express & Star*, Dave Woodhall from the Heroes & Villains website and Rob Bishop from Aston Villa FC for their help and advice.

I can honestly say, if it was not for the fans, the former players and everyone else who has kindly contributed to this project then I would not have been able to compile a book of this size. Thank you to everyone who is mentioned in the book.

Up the Villa!

Simon Goodyear

Aston Villa Old Stars

Founded 1960
52 consecutive years of fundraising fixtures

The Aston Villa Old Stars team has played up to 25 fundraising matches every year throughout the UK, in Ireland, the Channel Islands, Cyprus, Holland, France, Spain and Germany.

Since 1960, the names of the former players to have appeared in the Aston Villa Old Stars team reads like an Aston Villa Who's Who? The following is just a small selection of the great names to have represented the team since its formation:-

Charlie Aitken	Peter Aldis	Ron Atkinson
Paul Birch	Andy Blair	John Burridge
Harry Burrows	Mush Callaghan	Larry Canning
Vic Crowe	Frank Carrodus	Jim Cumbes
George Cummings	Alan Deakin	John Deehan
Johnny Dixon	Dickie Dorsett	Jimmy Dugdale
Trevor Ford	John Gidman	Brian Godfrey
Andy Gray	Chico Hamilton	Eric Houghton
Steve Hunt	Brian Little	Stan Lynn
Jimmy MacEwan	Johnny MacLeod	Con Martin
Bobby McDonald	Peter McParland	Sammy Morgan
Dennis Mortimer	Frank Moss	Chris Nicholl
Ian Olney	Harry Parkes	Leighton Phillips
Chris Price	Bruce Rioch	Ken Roberts
John Robson	Joe Rutherford	Davie Rudge
Pat Saward	Jackie Sewell	Gary Shaw
Nigel Sims	John Sleeuwenhoek	Gordon Smith
Leslie Smith	Simon Stainrod	Bobby Thomson
Mike Tindall	Fred Turnbull	Peter Withe

Added to these are the players in the current squad:
* denotes international and/or major trophy winner

*Chris Nicholl (Mgr)	*Des Bremner	*Stan Collymore
*Gordon Cowans	*Neil Cox	*Tony Daley
*Mark Delaney	*Mark Draper	*Dion Dublin
*Ugo Ehiogu	*Allan Evans	*Gareth Farrelly
*Steve Froggatt	*Colin Gibson	*Pat Heard
*Mark Jones	*Tommy Johnson	*Mark Kinsella
*Ivor Linton	*Paul Merson	*Tony Morley
*Gavin McCann	*Ken McNaught	*Brendan Ormsby
*Cyrille Regis	*Kevin Richardson	*Dean Saunders

*Nigel Spink   *Steve Staunton   *Kenny Swain
*Ian Taylor   *Shaun Teale   *Mark Walters
*Gary Williams   Dale Belford   Mark Blake
Darren Bradley   Mark Burke   John Capaldi
Martin Carruthers   Andy Comyn   Derek Dudley
Phil King   Dave Norton   Jon Pearson
Ben Petty   Gavin Price   Neil Rioch
Phil Robinson   Bryan Small   Gary Stirland
Garry Thompson   Ian Ward

Many of these former professional footballers have achieved the highest honours available in the game, and in today's multi-billion-pound professional football environment it is highly commendable to see so many great players giving their time and commitment in support of a deserving cause.

The Aston Villa Old Stars team has helped to raise well over £4½ million for charitable and deserving causes and they are, without doubt, the leading former players' team in the UK.

From left to right – Tony Morley, Pat Heard, Ken McNaught, Gordon Cowans and Colin Gibson were all in the 1982 European Cup-winning squad. Here they are wearing the kit of the Aston Villa Old Stars in 2010.

Aston Villa Former Players Association
Founded 1995

Formed in January 1995 to provide comprehensive representation, support and benefits to all of its members. It is governed by a Constitution within its Articles of Association and managed by former players and others.

Since our formation, the Aston Villa FPA has continued to help many former players and their families who have required assistance, be it medical, financial, educational, social, emotional or legal. This extensive health, welfare & well-being programme of delivery is and will remain, the core purpose of our existence.

The association continues to operate as a professional and effective organisation that is respected throughout the UK and as members of EFPA (European Group of Former Players Associations), in Europe also.

In addition to our core purpose, the AVFPA provides the platform for members to renew and make new friendships through its annual calendar of sporting, social and commercial activities, which includes:-

Aston Villa Old Stars football team (established in 1960)
Golf days & 'Ryder Cup' style golf matches
Cricket matches
'Legends' greyhound racing nights
Reunion & tribute dinners
Reciprocal links & support with Aston Villa Football Club
Business partnerships
Commercial enterprises

Plus other activities that have reunited over 400 former players from all over the world.

Whilst participating in many of these activities and events, former players are also supporting a primary objective of the Aston Villa FPA, which is our commitment to raising funds for charities and worthy causes, and nearly £5 million has been raised to date.

Aston Villa Football Club has a proud history and a bright future and the former players continue to support both with distinction. For more information, please log on to – **www.astonvillafpa.org** – or contact us direct by telephone on:

0844 873 5670 or by email to **info@astonvillafpa.org**

MIDLANDS MEMORABILIA
www.midlandsmemorabilia.com

Official memorabilia partners of the Aston Villa Former Players Association
Midlands Memorabilia stock a large range of items celebrating the rich history of Aston Villa. All signed items have been produced in association with our business partners Aston Villa Former Players Association.

www.midlandsmemorabilia.com

Midlands Memorabilia are one of the main business partners for AVFPA and the owner, Danny Drewry, travelled up and down Britain and Ireland over a three-week period in May 2011 trying to arrange a signing with every single Villa player who took part in the 1980–81 League Championship squad and the 1982 European Cup squad. He managed to arrange a meeting with every one of the 19 players involved in the two squads, and a replica shirt was signed by each of the following players:-

Jimmy Rimmer
Nigel Spink
Gary Williams
Colin Gibson
Eamon Deacy
Kenny Swain
Des Bremner
Allan Evans
Ken McNaught
Gordon Cowans
Tony Morley
Gary Shaw
Peter Withe
Andy Blair
Pat Heard
Brendon Ormbsby
Ivor Linton
David Geddis
Terry Donovan

This was a first for Midlands Memorabilia, being the only company to get all 19 players autographs on a replica shirt. The rare shirt is framed and appears on the Midlands Memorabilia website, selling for around £375.

Introduction

'Some people believe that football is a matter of life and death. I am very disappointed with that attitude, it is much, much more important than that!' With those words in mind, former Liverpool manager Bill Shankly inadvertently alluded to a new reality; football is not just a game. Well, in the most literal sense, football is obviously just a game and most people would have a hard time proving that it adds up to any more than 22 (over paid) players running around in pursuit of a round leather (or synthetic) object filled with air, while a lot more people (the fans) scream at them to do better. To be purely rational about it, football is nothing more or less than a game; you might add that these days it is an over-marketed, over-hyped, over-analysed one at that, and even its most ardent fan would agree with that. If that is the case, it is a game with such an extraordinary hold over the emotions that your melodramatic reaction maybe fully justified. So the question is why do we love football so much, and more to the point why do we support Aston Villa? Why do we put ourselves through the cyclic years of mediocrity followed by periods when our team seem to be world beaters? As the entertainer and celebrity Villa fan Dave Ismay puts it, 'To follow the Villa is an encapsulation of life itself. You experience every human emotion, sentiment, feeling or passion that life has to offer and too often it seems, within the same game. The enigmatic "claret and blues" can nevertheless take you to unparalleled highs of adrenalin rush to unplumbed depths of unbearable grief and despondency. Nothing is ever mundane and ordinary and from as far back as my fading memory permits my moods have been governed by their results.'

Of course he's spot on with his analogy.

In the old days, before Sky TV and the internet, people used to support the football club they were born closest to or would follow their father's favourite team. Today, the fashion is to support glamorous teams riding high in the Premier League. These people are more commonly known as 'glory hunters'. Of course, football fans from the 'old school' have always insisted on a 'football birthright', being born or at least living within a few miles of the ground to qualify as a replica-shirt-wearing true supporter. Historically, it was always said that the North Birmingham, Sutton Coldfield and Tamworth areas were generally considered to be populated by Villa fans, and generally speaking this still holds true today.

I'm not entirely sure why my late father, David Goodyear, chose to be a Villa fan, but his passion for the club throughout his life was plain to see as he fulfilled his dreams of not only writing several books on his beloved club but to actually work for the club as a match day steward and as the club's Historian and Archivist for many years. He was also the Secretary for the Aston Villa Former Players Association for several years and he was privileged enough to meet some of his own Villa 'heroes'. What my father did not know about Villa you could probably write on a postage stamp. Among his favourites players included Tommy Thompson, Gerry Hitchens (incidentally, being the subject of my first book), Brian Little and Gary Shaw. I think he had a soft spot for Savo as well. With a father who had claret and blue blood there was no way I was going to support any other club than Aston Villa was there, especially not the local rivals from Small Heath!

My own memories of first going to Villa Park go as far back as 1971–72 season, and I distinctly remember the names Charlie Aitken, Bruce Rioch, Chico Hamilton, Ray Graydon and a bald-headed striker called Andy Lochhead, who at the time must have been about 30 years old but I thought looked a distinctly old 40 (well I was only seven years old at the time). Those of us who remember that year, it was when the club was on its knees and in the third tier of English football under Vic Crowe. The names I have mentioned were great players, and for the club and having a team of such quality in the Third Division was a travesty. Some say that these were 'dark days' for the club, but there is also an argument that they were 'special' times. I will always remember the big crowds in those days; we would get over 40,000 against teams like Walsall, Bristol Rovers and 48,000 against Bournemouth as we stormed to win the title and got to Wembley in 1971.

Then came the Ron Saunders era, and I was well into football by then and excited by the prospect of a new revolution at the club with players like Chris Nicholl, Brian Little and Andy Gray coming in. Gray was my own boyhood football hero (and probably still is). I loved his lion heart spirit, and he always seemed to score goals every time dad and I went down to Villa Park. We also took in a few trips to Wembley along the way, but by the time of the 1980–81 season, dad and I travelled up and down the country following the lads and we were among the 25,000 Brummies at Highbury on 2 May 1981, packed in behind the goal in the Clock End, the day football came home. The following season was even better as the one of the most famous names in football became European champions. Can you imagine how special that year was? It was also special because it was the year I left school! However, during the mid-1980s I was turned off football, along with the masses, because of the ugly scenes that were all too frequent at football grounds all over England.

More recently, the games that stick out in my memory include the 5–1 against Blues in 2008 and the Blackburn League Cup semi-final. Those games for me epitomised the style of football we Villa fans want to watch week in, week out but all too frequently, fail to deceive.

Football today has changed beyond recognition, but to me it's just as exciting – maybe even more so as the prizes and the pressure are so much greater than ever before. It provides a passion never seen before, even if the pride has disappeared to some extent. The quality and professionalism of football are obvious pluses but the vast amounts players get paid now seem to have put a barrier between the fan and the player, which was never there years ago. More often or not, (some) players shun the chance to give their adoring fans even an autograph, let alone a photo with them. Not only that, I, along with almost every other football fan of my generation and before, would agree the all-seater stadium probably takes away some of the spark and atmosphere there used to be years ago behind the Holte End; however, on the big occasions, like for those European nights or Cup ties, the atmosphere can be quite electric.

As soon as I had the idea for this book in my head I was excited at the prospect of producing something which would (hopefully) appeal to several generations of fans, from people whose memories span as far back as the 1920s right up to the modern day fan who only know Premier League football and Sky TV. To me, the thought of producing such a unique book was appealing because there are so many products out there which are a 'much of a muchness' and I wanted to compile a book which would be a bit 'different' but at the same time, be informative and interesting and would have vast appeal to all ages.

Some of the topics in the book you may have seen before in different places but I have tried to put a different spin on them, especially the historical section; the poems are all genuine and original and although they may not appeal to some people at first, they are all Villa related and I think give another dimension to the book and I hope provide a bit of cultural education. I sourced the poems from various places and sought permission from the authors directly to publish them in this book. Personally, I think they are interesting and add a bit of diversification from the rest of the book.

Having the opportunity of interviewing the former players included in the book was a privilege and an honour for me and I am very grateful to the Aston Villa Former Players Association for allowing me access to the former players. Some of the guys like Gary Shaw and Tony Morley I have met many times before but some I haven't and all were willing to share their memories with me. Their stories should give the book a wider appeal and I am sure you will be keen to read their recollections of days gone by. Talking to the likes of Gary Shaw, Tony Morley, Ken McNaught and Pat Heard about that day in May 1982 was to me very special as these were my heroes I watched and loved 30 years ago. These are the same players who were given no chance before the Final but competed with the best and came away with the biggest prize in domestic football and their names will forever remain in Aston Villa folklore history.

Simon Goodyear

There's Only One Aston Villa

There are many teams called 'United', 'City', 'Town' or 'County' and a few called 'Wanderers' and 'Rovers' and even some with the name 'Albion' after it, but thank God there's only one 'Aston Villa' – probably the greatest name of them all. It was the name 'Aston Villa' that Hollywood star Tom Hanks apparently fell in love with, 'Years ago, I saw the name Aston Villa float by on my TV screen and liked the name. In the life of every football fan, there comes a time when you have to declare your allegiance.' Not only that, former Villa manager, John Gregory, was once quoted as saying, 'There's an aura about this club, a sense of history and tradition. Even the name is beautifully symmetrical, with five letters in each word.' I think every Villa fan will agree that the club has a great history and a certain aura and aristocracy about it that our rivals just do not have.

I have tried to narrow down some of the most memorable periods in history and some of the best games ever seen at Villa Park, together with a sprinkling of other notable years that have made the club what it is today. Some of you will remember these times like it was just yesterday and some obviously too far back in history for anyone alive to recall; however, if you know anything about your Villa history, you will have heard of or maybe remembered some of the following events which changed the club's fortunes, for better or for worse. This is not meant to be a history lesson – those books have been written superbly many times before, but more of a step back in time with a few facts and figures thrown in for good measure.

☉

1874

A milestone all Villa fans should know. Some members of the Male Adult Bible Class met at the Aston Villa Wesleyan Chapel in Handsworth and talked about forming a football club for their winter activity. One of the members, William B. Mason, played in a rugby match a few days later and after the match, a group of members consisting of Mason, along with John Hughes, George Matthews, William H. Price and William Scattergood met under a gas-light in Heathfield Road to discuss the possibility of forming a club with slightly different rules to rugby. From that day on, the name 'Aston Villa' was adopted.

Wilson Road, Birchfield, Birmingham Aston Villa's first official game took place here in March 1875, beating local rugby team Aston Brook St Mary's 1–0.

1887

In the FA Cup first round, Villa scored 13 goals against Wednesbury Old Athletic to create a record victory which still stands today. This was followed by a 6–1 victory over Derby Midland. Villa reached their first Final and played West Bromwich Albion at Kennington Oval in London. Albion were firm favourites, but Villa beat their local rivals 2–0 to win their first-ever trophy.

1888

On Tuesday 17 April 1888, Aston Villa Director William McGregor held a meeting with around 12 of the most prominent clubs in England, including Villa, and the Football League was duly formed.

1894

Villa were champions for the first time as they toppled Sunderland by six points. Sunderland were the previous year's winners and had a strong side in those days.

1895

The FA Cup trophy was stolen from a Birmingham shop window following Villa's second Cup victory. A £10 reward was offered for its retrieval but it was never found.

1896

League champions for a second time, winning 20 out of the 30 games in the process in the 1895–96 season.

1897

In a momentous year for Aston Villa as the club moved from Wellington Road, Perry Barr to a new stadium in Aston Lower Grounds (now called Villa Park). This was a significant step for the club and showed the progress it had made since its formation.

On the pitch, Villa won their third League title and secured their only ever double by winning the FA Cup again. That achievement would not be repeated until 1961, when that great Tottenham Hotspur side won the League and Cup double. The list of clubs who have won the double is like the bijou list of English clubs who have won the European Cup and retains a small, elite feel. However, Villa boast one distinction that will never be matched – they won both trophies on the same day. This is because Derby County, the only other team who could have caught Villa, went down to Bury and that defeat effectively ruined their Championship ambitions.

1899

Villa won another the League Championship, the fourth in six years.

1900
For the second time, Villa retained the First Division title.

1905
Villa won the FA Cup for the fourth time, with Harry Hampton scoring two goals against Newcastle United in front of over 100,000 fans.

1906
With the club well formed and winning trophies for fun, a new match day programme was published for the first time by Edwin W. Cox, a well-known sports journalist at the time. It was called the *Aston Villa News & Record* and was in black and white until the first colour editions surfaced in the early 1970s. In 2006, it celebrated its 100th birthday and has won many accolades over the years.

Villa Park c.1907.

1910
Villa were seen as relegation candidates, but they defied the odds and won the First Division Championship for the 6th time (and the last time for the next 70 years).

1911
With the team rebuilding the club purchase Aston Lower Grounds (Villa Park). However, everything was overshadowed by the death of William McGregor.

1913
The club's directors approved the expansion of Villa Park at the 1913 AGM. They wanted a ground which would hold 120,000 people but unfortunately, a year later, 'The Great War' got in the way and the plans were shelved.

However, just before the 'Great War', Villa recorded their fifth FA Cup win by beating Sunderland 1–0 in front of a crowd of 121,919 at The Crystal Palace, a record attendance to watch a Villa game.

1920
Four years without a League match, due to the 'Great War', Villa yet again lifted the FA Cup by beating favourites Huddersfield Town in the final, but only after extra-time.

1927

Villa fans have always had a love affair with strikers, and the arrival of Tranmere Rovers forward, Tom 'Pongo' Waring captured the fans imagination like no other player in the club's history. The fee of £4,700 was a record at the time and Waring duly repaid the club's faith in him by scoring a hat-trick on his debut in a reserve match which attracted a crowd of 23,000.

1931

'Pongo' Waring scores 50 League goals as Villa finished runners-up to Arsenal in a record-breaking season which saw Villa score 128 League goals – still a top-flight record – including a magnificent 86 goals scored at Villa Park, but they still did not lift a trophy.

1936

Blackburn and Villa, two of the original members of the Football League, were relegated for the first time in their history. However, the fans still turned out in their thousands and 41,000 saw Villa in their first home game in Division Two.

1938

With Villa crowned Second Division champions, and World War Two looming, they took part in a three-match tour of Germany (of all places). In a game against a Germany Select XI at the Reichssportfeld (the Olympic Stadium) in Berlin, 110,000 people saw Villa win 3–2 under the watchful eye of Adolf Hitler.

After only one season out of the top flight, Villa were promoted. They settled back into life in the First Division and the crowds followed their every move, with over 1 million people watching their first team games at Villa Park. Villa were back in the 'big time.'

1946

It was a period of rebuilding again for Villa following the war in an attempt to achieve honours. With the Football League restored after the war, 50,000 saw the opening game of the 1946–47 season and 76,588 saw Villa lose to Derby County in the FA Cup sixth round (and it remains the biggest crowd ever to see a home game at Villa Park). Some of the team that played in the last game before the war in 1939, the likes of Iverson, Rutherford and Cummings were joined by new signings like Johnny Dixon, Trevor Ford and Harry Parkes.

1948 – A game to remember – Villa 4 Manchester United 6

There were hopes in the new year of 1948 that Villa would be good bets for the FA Cup, but Manchester United had other ideas in their third-round tie. George Edwards gave the home side the perfect start within the first minute but it all fell apart after that as United battered the Villa defence with five goals before half-time in front of nearly 59,000 fans. However, Villa staged a near incredible fight back in the second period to bring the score to a more respectable 4–5 until a sixth United goal effectively killed the game. It is a game that will live in the memory of all Villa fans of that era if not for the result but for pure excitement.

1957

With Villa languishing in the relegation zone for much of the previous season, who would have expected them to reach the FA Cup Final in 1957 let alone win it? However, their League form was inconsistent, even though there was an improvement on the previous season as Villa finished 10th. The famous Villa triumph in the FA Cup of 1957 gave Midland's football a

huge lift, but it didn't do much to alleviate the inconsistent results which the fans demanded. Villa 'legend' Peter McParland took his tally to seven goals in the competition as he scored a brace to beat the 'Busby Babes' 2–1 at Wembley.

The 1957 FA Cup-winners.

1959 – A game to remember – Villa 11 Charlton Athletic 1

This incredible match will be long remembered as Aston Villa's highest-ever League score in the post-war era and was the highlight of the 1959–60 season, which saw Villa win the Second Division Championship. Goals came almost as frequently as the raindrops and helped excite the poor 22,000 crowd at a cold Villa Park. Gerry Hitchens was at that time a much criticised centre-forward and was nearly dropped for this match by manager Eric Houghton, but he scored the first five of six goals on that day.

Villa began well with a goal from Hitchens within the first two minutes. It was the first goal in five appearances for the centre-forward. Charlton scored an equaliser in the 22nd minute but Bobby Thomson scored a second Villa goal in the 26th minute, his first goal in ten games. At this point it looked as though Charlton were going to give Villa a game. Villa's third goal was scored by Hitchens in the 29th minute. The goalkeeper, Duff, saved from Thomson but he couldn't hold the ball and Hitchens dashed in to score as the defenders stood and watched, dismayed by his opportunism. This really demoralised Charlton and led to their demise in the game. Five minutes later, Hitchens struck another blow to the Londoners five minutes before half-time when he nipped in to score his hat-trick, as the Charlton defenders stood and watched in mysterious contemplation. At half-time the score was 4–1 to Villa. After the break, Villa continued in the same vein and Hitchens demonstrated to the full the inefficiencies of the Charlton defence by picking up the ball from a Villa goal kick and running on to score without another player touching the ball. The centre-forward hooked in his fifth goal in the 60th minute and when the Charlton 'keeper, Duff, went off with a damaged finger with Villa leading 6–1, the home team were still hungry for more goals.

After Duff went off, Charlton tried two deputy 'keepers but neither had much success. In the following ten minutes, Villa scored a further three goals through Wylie, Thomson (with his second) and MacEwan. Peter McParland scored Villa's 10th goal in the 72nd minute and it wasn't until the 86th minute that the 11th and final goal went in, again through McParland to claim his second of the game. It was a great finale to one of the biggest Villa League successes ever, secured by the individualism of Hitchens and the collective opportunism and intelligence of the Villa midfield.

1961

Back in the top flight after only a season away and 'Mercer's Minors' cemented themselves in the top half, but would it last? This was meant to be the start of a new dawn.

Villa began their love affair with the Football League Cup by beating Rotherham United over two legs (and over two seasons) in the inaugural campaign.

Gerry Hitchens left for Inter Milan for a club record transfer sale of £85,000, but not before he scored an incredible 42 goals in the 1960–61 season, including 11 in the League Cup campaign, even though he didn't play in the Final. Another Villa icon, Johnny Dixon, retired after the last game of the season and it was Charlie Aitken's debut in the same game against Sheffield Wednesday.

1968

After eight seasons of mediocrity and relegation to Division Two, new Chairman, Doug Ellis promised a revolution at the club. However, it started poorly and fans revolted from the start and a poor run of results led to the sacking of Tommy Cummings. Another Tommy took over. This time it was the enigmatic Tommy Docherty but unfortunately from then on, the club would unfortunately soon sink to new lows.

1974

Ron Saunders was installed at the helm, replacing Vic Crowe in the summer of 1974 after briefly managing Manchester City. Even though Villa were still in the Second Division, there was renewed hope and rightly so, as Saunders steered the club back into the top flight in his first season in charge, coming runners up to Manchester United, followed by another League Cup win in the same season and finally a new era seemed to be is dawning (again).

1975
Villa won the League Cup for the third time and also competed in Europe for the first time in the club's history but it was a short lived adventure as they were knocked out in the first round of the UEFA Cup.

1976 – A game to remember – Villa 5 Liverpool 1
Perhaps the biggest frustration of being a Villa fan is that classic seasons tend to be one-offs and we look forward to the next season with keen interest, only to be disappointed. We also see lots of good teams being developed by numerous managers but seldom develop into great ones. No line-up demonstrated this infuriating tendency better than the men who rampaged through the First Division in 1976–77 but then faded from view as quickly as they had emerged. There are Villa fans of a certain age who believe that this was a better team in many respects than 1981 Championship team or even the 1982 European Cup team. It was another Ron Saunders team that played fast, high octane attacking football built on an athleticism that was years ahead of its time that won the 1977 League Cup. They reached the quarter-finals of the FA Cup and finished fourth in the First Division, smashing goal after spectacular goal past the best teams in the land with arguably one of the strongest strike forces the club has ever seen.

The match of the season took place on 15 December 1976 when the champions of England, Liverpool (who went onto win the First Division title and the European Cup that same season), were humbled by Saunders's attack minded side by 5–1 with all the goals coming in perhaps the most memorable first 45 minutes in Villa Park history in front of nearly 43,000.

1977
Villa beat Everton 3–2 at Old Trafford to win the League Cup after two breathtaking replays. The first match at Wembley finished goalless and the second finished in a 1–1 draw at Hillsborough, but it was left to Brian Little to win the tie for Villa with just four minutes left in the game.

In the UEFA Cup, Villa got to the fourth round where they were unlucky to lose against Spanish giants Barcelona in front of 80,000 at the Camp Neu.

1981
With Doug Ellis no longer chairman of the club and, after a few seasons of stability with Ron Saunders in charge of the team, Villa unexpectedly won the League for the first time since the 1909–10 season. Not bad for a team who the London based media gave no credit (and no chance) all through

the season. After Ipswich had beaten Villa in April 1981 to put themselves into pole position, Ron Saunders put his neck on the block by saying to the media, 'Do you want to bet against us?'

It all hinged on the last game of the season at Highbury but results elsewhere proved more important than the result against Arsenal as 25,000 Villa fans saw a 2–0 defeat, but it didn't matter in the end as news filtered through that Ipswich had lost to Middlesbrough and the name Bosko Jankovic would remain in Villa folklore history forever.

1982

As 'champions of England', Villa did not live up to their billing in the next League campaign as they only managed to finish 11th. However, as Ron Saunders unexpectedly left Villa Park to hand over the reins to Tony Barton midway through the season who would have expected Villa to overcome the mighty Bayern Munich and be crowned 'Champions of Europe' on 26 May 1982 as Peter Withe's famous 'mis-kick' was the difference between the two sides on that famous night in Rotterdam.

In January 1983, Villa beat Barcelona over two legs to win the European Super Cup and also competed in the World Club Championship in Tokyo but finished runners up and Doug Ellis returned to the club as chairman for the second time.

1986

Disillusioned fans stayed away from Villa Park, in their thousands (and from football in general) as the aftermath of Heysel kicked in. Villa's average gate for the season was only 15,237, the lowest since the 'Great War'. Football was at its knees and the once 'Kings of Europe' were facing mediocrity once again.

After being 'champions of Europe' only a few seasons before and 12 seasons in the First Division Villa were relegated under Billy McNeill and the club was in turmoil once again.

1988

Villa gained promotion back to the First Division at the first attempt but it was tight as it went down to the wire with David Platt scoring the only goal against Bradford City at Villa Park in the penultimate game of the season.

1991

Another 'new dawn' starts as 'Big' Ron Atkinson starts his flamboyant reign as Villa manager and rings in the changes on and off the field. 'Big Ron' brought 'Champagne Football' to Villa Park and saw the crowds return at last after the 1980s slump in the year before football changed forever.

1992

The breakaway FA Premier League was formed in 1992 and again Villa were founder members of the 'elite' League. Ron Atkinson's era got off to a wonderful start as his team finished second behind Manchester United, but 10 points adrift as Villa lost their last three games of the season.

1994 – A game to remember – Villa 3 Tranmere Rovers 2

When the draw for the Coca-Cola Cup semi-finals in 1994 paired Villa with Tranmere Rovers some Villa fans were already making their Wembley travel arrangements. But in the first leg at Prenton Park, Tranmere were a team inspired while Villa were at best, dreadful and the underdogs beat 'Big Ron's' giants by 3–1; however, that away goal scored by Dalian Atkinson with the last kick of the game, gave Villa a glimmer of hope for the return leg. Then one Sunday in February found Villa Park packed to the rafters for the club's most dramatic match of the modern era. Villa raced into a 2–0 lead inside 23 minutes and the fans hopes were raised. Then John Aldridge pulled one back from a penalty with goalkeeper Mark Bosnich lucky not to have been sent off and Tranmere were back in charge again. There were no more goals until, two minutes from time, Atkinson headed in Tony Daley's cross to produce a roar of terrifying volume and intensity and sent the match into extra-time. No more goals in extra-time and it was down to nerve-wracking penalties. In goalkeeper, Mark Bosnich, the brash and brilliant young Aussie, Villa had just the man for the moment. He saved three brilliantly and after a match that sapped the emotions of all the 40,593 fans present, Villa were on their way back to Wembley.

1996

Undoubtedly the best season in many years, Brian Little's side won another League Cup at Wembley after beating Leeds convincingly 3–0. Not only that, they finished fourth in the Premier League and reached the semi-final of the FA Cup. It seemed the fans were right – Brian Little did walk on water after all.

2000

Villa reached their first FA Cup Final since 1957 but go down 1–0 to Chelsea at 'the old Wembley' in one of the least entertaining Finals for many a year. It was the last Cup Final ever to be played there before it was demolished and rebuilt. Furthermore, it was also the year that the famous old Trinity Road stand was demolished. Since 1923 the mighty red-brick structure with its stained glass windows and gorgeous Italian marble mosaics had come to represent Aston Villa and was for many the most globally recognised symbol of the club but Villa had to move with the times and a wonderful new main stand, fit for the 21st century replaced the out-of-date but iconic Trinity Road stand.

2001
Villa's season started in mid-July as they had to qualify for Europe by winning the UEFA InterToto Cup, which they did. Under manager John Gregory, Villa spent big that season but still only finished 8th in the Premier League.

2006
A brand new era was awaiting Martin O'Neill as he was appointed as the new manager in August 2006 and crowds flocked to greet him. Soon afterwards, American billionaire businessman and self-proclaimed Villa fan Randy Lerner took over the stewardship of the club from Doug Ellis.

2008 – A game to remember – Villa 5 Birmingham City 1
Expectations for the 2007–08 season were at a near all-time high and over 36,000 turned up for a pre-season friendly game against Inter Milan. League attendances soared to a 58-year high and the team were good value for a top six finish but failed again in both Cup competitions.

However, on 20th April 2008, a live TV audience were witnessed to one of the best games of football from a Villa side for many a year against a struggling Birmingham City side (who were to be relegated). Goals were free flowing in the period leading up to this local derby but who would have expected such an explosion of goals and such wonderful football from the home side.

Villa were in control from the kick off but it took half an hour to break the deadlock as Ashley Young drove the ball into the bottom corner. Just before half-time, John Carew glanced a header past Maik Taylor and the game was virtually over when Carew tapped in for his second. Young made it four shortly after and Forssell scored a consolation goal to narrow the margin until Gabby Agbonlahor fired home to make it 5–1 in the 77th minute to seal the rout. That goal prompted a mass exodus by those Blues fans who hadn't already gone home before half-time. It was a very special day indeed.

2009
Villa again finished 6th in the 2008–09 season and Ashley Young was named PFA Young Player of the Year and the club seemed to be stable and on the up.

2010 – A game to remember – Villa 6 Blackburn Rovers 4
Ten years since the last trip to Wembley and another Final beckoned after a narrow 1–0 semi-final first leg win at Ewood Park. This game had everything but as usual the team put their fans through every type of emotion in the book. **Despair** – within half an hour, the visitors had a two-goal lead. **Tension** – at half-time, Villa were level and had one foot in the

final. **Exhilaration** – suddenly, it was 5–2 as Emile Heskey fired home in front of the Holte End and the 40,000 crowd thought it was all over. Then – no, surely they can't get back into it, can they? Ten-men Blackburn defied the odds by hitting two goals back to make it 5–4 on the night and reduced the aggregate deficit to two. **Euphoria** – Ashley Young coolly put away the sixth and put the game to bed and saw his side home and Villa were finally booking their places to Wembley.

2010

Villa enjoyed another campaign to remember, finishing sixth once again and beat some of the best teams in the League along the way. The team reached the League Cup Final and FA Cup semi-final, but in August 2010 Martin O'Neill stunned the Villa faithful (and the football world) by announcing his resignation, two weeks before the start of the season.

In September 2010, Gerard Houllier was appointed his replacement.

2011

Darren Bent became Villa's record-breaking signing in a reported £24 million deal, doubling the previous record captures of James Milner and Stuart Downing. In what was considered a poor season, Villa finished the season well and climbed to ninth in the Premier League. In June 2011 Gerard Houllier resigned after less than one season due to ill-health.

Alex McCleish is appointed manager after resigning from neighbours Birmingham City and within his first few weeks saw the departures of Villa favourite Ashley Young to Manchester United, and then Stewart Downing left for Liverpool in mid-July.

Thanks For The Memories

Everyone has their favourite memory or a great story they want to tell, even if they don't realise it. I have heard so many stories from Villa fans and former players over the years that I as soon as I had the idea for this project, I knew that there would be enough material to fill a decent-sized book. The alternative was that these great stories would remain implanted in people's heads forever, never to be told and that would have been such a shame.

The funny thing about researching for this book was that alot of people did not realise that they had anything to say or any memories of matches or stories of being a Villa fan which they thought worth talking about until that is, they actually started talking. I found this was generally the case as I randomly interviewed some Villa fans and the response was usually, 'I don't have any memories really...' A few minutes later, some wonderful stories unfolded from the deepest depths of their memory cells. Some people didn't consider their own memories as being of interest to anyone else but to me, and I'm sure to you the reader, these memories I have captured in this chapter and the forthcoming sections are the wonderful interpretations of everyday people going about their life and how they spent their days supporting this great club through all the good times and even through the bad times. All of these events that have been captured here will never happen again so I think that makes these stories more interesting to read and even more important to have captured them. All of the pieces written in the following pages are words taken from the people who contacted me and not my own words.

⚽

Peter McParland was a forward who played for Villa from 1952 to 1962 and was famous for scoring the two goals that beat the famous 'Busby Babes' of Manchester United in the 1957 FA Cup Final. I interviewed Peter, and he recalled a couple of contrasting memories of his times at Villa.

The biggest disappointment I can remember while playing football was to be relegated from the First Division in 1959. I was a member of that team when we played West Bromwich Albion at The Hawthorns in the last game of the season. We drew 1–1 and we went down to the Second Division. I remember I had the ball in my hand in order to take a quick corner, and the final whistle went before I could take it. That immediate moment the whistle was blown my heart just sank and I dropped like a stone. It was a big, big disappointment. After the game as I recall, on the bus back to Villa Park it was very sombre. I went straight home I think but some people say that a party had been arranged in Edgbaston, but I don't remember that. Afterwards, looking back at it all, the season was such that we had a good run in the FA Cup, reaching the semi-final but we lost to Nottingham Forest at Hillsborough on the Saturday and on the

30

Peter McParland scoring for Villa in the 1957 FA Cup Final.

Tuesday night going up to Bolton and beating The Trotters convincingly 3–1, who were a hard, tough side at the time. Then, little things turned against us in the run in towards the end of the season and everything hung on the last game at The Hawthorns.

The other teams involved in the dog fight at the foot of the table, Leicester City and Manchester City were playing each other on the last day so it was imperative that we won, otherwise we would go down. As it turned out, we drew with West Brom and both Leicester and Manchester City escaped the drop. We were relegated along with Portsmouth (as only two teams were relegated in those days). There was never the feeling in the side that we were 'too good to go down' but after the Bolton result and the disappointment of losing in the semi-final, in a game we should have at least got a replay in, we were feeling pretty confident but unfortunately, on the day, we did not win and were relegated.

I would say it was the biggest disappointment that I have encountered in football and I'm sure all the players who were in that team on that evening felt the same. As it happens, I was involved in another relegation fight (in 1955–56) in another Vila side (and survived) but we were a far superior side in 1959 and still went down.

With the disappointment of relegation, it was a case of having a break and then pick ourselves up for the next season. As it happened, the mood from the start of the season was good and we just seemed to get on with it and started winning and got ourselves to the top of the League. We battled our way through from there and we were always in the top two or three throughout the season. There was a period of time when we had a nine or 10 point gap leading up to the end of the season and the only team who could catch us were Cardiff City, who eventually came only a point behind us at the end of the season as we had a wee bit of a blip towards the end.

However, in contrast, the biggest satisfaction I've ever encountered was early in the next season, after we had gained promotion back to the First Division, going to The Hawthorns and giving them a good hiding 2–0. Ronnie Allen, who scored in that game on the last day of the 1958–59 season, always bragged that he had scored the goal that sent the Villa down. We gained sweet revenge and beat The Albion and Ronnie got more than a few touches that day from our lads (and it wasn't of the ball!). I think you'd call it 'just deserts'? There were about 41,000 at The Hawthorns on that day and I bet there were around 35,000 Villa fans wanting to watch us gain 'revenge' and they were lucky enough to see it. It was like a home game to us with the support we had from the Villa fans.

Peter McParland, former Villa forward 1952–62.

Tony Morley holding the European Cup aloft after the 1982 Final.

An ever present on the left wing for the hugely successful Villa team of the early 1980s, Tony Morley helped the club win the 1980–81 First Division title in only his second season, scoring the 1981 Goal of the Season along the way. Even greater success was to come in the following season, when the club lifted the European Cup at the first attempt. Morley was to play a vital part in the Final, his typically pacy run and left footed cross setting up Peter Withe to score the winner against the much fancied Bayern Munich side. Playing the best football of his career, Morley went on to make 180 appearances for Villa, scoring 34 times. He also won a Super Cup medal with the team in 1983.

The flying winger is now a prominent member of the Aston Villa Former Players Association and a regular player in the 'Aston Villa Old Stars' team. He has also provided match commentary for radio broadcasts on the official Aston Villa website and is also an ambassador for Football Aid.

In this piece, Tony talks about his 'wonder' goal against his boyhood club, Everton on 7 February 1981, Ron Saunders and about European Cup glory.

A lot of people think I was being rude to Ron Saunders when I gestured to him, but what people don't realise is that at Bodymoor Heath on the Friday before the game he put me in the reserves in the 'defensive wall' so when you got the yellow shirt you always knew you were in the 'wall' and the first eleven took free kicks against you. So I said to Ron, 'Am I not playing?' I was not interested in his reply. All I wanted to hear was that I was in the team to face my team Everton. He did not reply, anyway. When I went off the pitch after training I was absolutely disgusted. I'd had a half decent season up until then and I couldn't understand why he was going to drop me.

Before the game on the Saturday, we went out for a meal at a hotel in Liverpool. Ron said nothing to me and I found out that Pat Heard was playing in place of me. In the dressing room, Ron turned round to me and said, 'Pat Heard's a bit too young and inexperienced, you're playing.' What he had done for over 24 hours was basically wind me up. All that frustration built up and that's why I went out onto the pitch in the first 10 minutes like a bull in a china shop and I wanted to prove a point to him. I scored the opener within the first 10 minutes (and it was voted Goal of the Season). The 'V' sign I made at Ron was out of pure frustration and was not meant to be malicious.

Ron had done his homework and didn't have to say anything to me. He knew all my friends and family would be there watching and he knew what he was doing. We had to win the game and get two points at all cost. He kept us on our toes at least. After the game he pulled me up about the silly gesture I made at him and fined me, 'You will go down as the player who won the game, but I'm fining you a week's wages for doing that sign at me.' It all went to charity so that was ok. That was Saunders all round. He was a total one-off. He would never praise me; I don't recall him ever praising me. There were three lads he would never praise – me, Gary Shaw and Gordon Cowans. I think he thought we had a bit more 'something' that could give a bit extra to the team and by being on top of us he would get the best out of us. It was not personal but his way of man managing. He had fantastic man management skills really to be fair. Saying all that about Ron, contrary to what people think, we were friends, but it doesn't mean we always got on.

He did the same in Berlin when I scored two goals (21 October 1981). He bet me on the morning of the game that I'd never score two goals because he thought I was 'too flash' and I'd try and curl them and this, that and the other, but once again I proved him wrong and scored two superb goals. Some people said I did the same after my second goal, giving him the 'V' sign but I was gesturing to him that I had scored two goals. He never said anything to me during or after the game. Incidentally, I won 'Goal of Europe' one of my goals in that game. A couple of weeks later, he pulled me up and said, 'That was the best game I've seen you play,' but then he fined me two weeks wages. I was not worried about being fined as my goals got us to the semi-finals of the European Cup.

When Ron Saunders left we were all in shock. Nobody had any idea he was about to leave. He had a coughing fit during a training session and the next thing we knew he'd left the club. I am adamant that if Ron had stayed on and had been given a new, longer contract Villa would have been 'the' team definitely in England, if not Europe. We were a far better side than Everton were who dominated in the mid-1980s. The problem was Doug Ellis came in shortly after the European win and changed everything and got rid of the likes of myself and Denis Mortimer. It was a shame as I felt sorry for the supporters. We only had 14 or 15 players and he sold five or six of them. I'd have loved to have a few more medals; it could have been a conveyor belt. It did not happen and that was that.

However, the Final itself, I don't remember much about really. It was crazy. Most people don't know this but we had a situation at Villa where a lot of the players were sponsored by Nike. So Nike offered the club X amount of money for some of the players to wear this new boot which they were launching. The club accepted and five or six of the players wore this new boot on the match day – the European Cup Final. It was absolutely ludicrous as these lads came off the pitch with huge blisters. I know Kenny Swain was one who wore the new boot. Alan Evans and Ken McNaught may have been others. These boots weren't like the boots they make now, all soft and light weight, they were hard and heavy and caused incredible blisters on the feet.

We knew we were a good side and would soak up all the pressure and that we would get no more than one chance in the game and it was proved right. We had one chance and we took it. Not many European finals are dominated by one team and that night was no exception. In a one-off game anything can happen as long as you keep disciplined and organised you have a chance of winning. We had Tony Barton at the helm. He was a lovely man but we found it hard at first to accept him as boss (following Ron Saunders' departure). Tony didn't expect us to call him 'boss'. He knew all the lads anyway inside out as he had been working with us day in day out and when he was a scout as well and probably knew us better than Ron did.

Tony Morley, former Villa winger, 1979–84.

Neil Rioch is the younger brother of Bruce Rioch, who also played for Villa in the 1970s. One of Neil's fondest memories was as a 15-year-old Luton Town apprentice and he was actually selected to take part in the 1966 World Cup Final, not as a player but as a ball boy. Not only that, he was in fact the first Englishman to touch the ball in that famous Final – now there's a quiz question. Neil talks about his debut for Villa in 1969 and about how he got involved in the Aston Villa Former Players Association.

My first game for Villa was a pre-season friendly played at Villa Park against an Italian Under-23 international XI in the summer of 1969 and we wore yellow shirts, royal blue shorts and yellow socks and when we ran out onto the pitch we were 'booed' by the home crowd because they thought we were the Italians, mainly because we all had good suntans.

However, my League debut was away at Huddersfield Town on 16th August 1969. On the way to the ground, Tommy Docherty said to me, 'You're playing today, son.' Huddersfield were a strong side (they went on to win the Second Division that season) so it was not the best team to make your debut against. I was given the task of marking their centre-forward, a one Frank Worthington. It was a tough debut.

Another game I remember was playing against Blackburn Rovers in October 1971 and I was playing at centre-half, and I scored two goals in a 4–1 victory. Both goals were scored at the Witton End. I did not play much that season or the next season but I scored the winner in a top of the table clash against Bristol City at the Holte End. I have many good memories of being at Villa but that was the greatest moment of my Villa career. I'll always treasure that one.

Some years ago, probably in about 1980, I got invited to play for the Aston Villa Old Stars. At the time I was already playing and running the Denis Waterman charity side, which I had been involved in for 11 years. In 1980–81 I played the odd game for the Villa Old Stars and with the

Waterman Charity XI finishing I was asked to play for the Old Stars on a regular basis after that.

In the early 1990s I was asked to take over the running of the side, organising the team and have been involved with it ever since. At the time I took over, it wasn't going so well as we couldn't get players to turn up. However, whilst I was running the side in the 1990s I read a newspaper article, possibly in the Sunday Mercury, about ex-Villa player Stan Lynn having to sell his 1957 FA Cup-winners medal just to make ends meet. Having read this it was something I couldn't come to terms with. Here we were, playing football matches to raise hundreds of thousands of pounds every year for good causes but what better cause was there than an ex-Villa legend having to sell his Cup-winners' medal. So that motivated me to start the Aston Villa Former Players Association in 1994 (launched in January 1995).

Today, 16 years later, it is going from strength to strength and now is widely recognised throughout Europe as the most advanced former players association. There is great support from the players themselves and from other people who help to manage the association. It is now my full-time job which I never dreamed it would be, 16 years ago.

Other clubs have looked at what we have done. In fact I have been invited to about 25 clubs to give them advice and guidance on how to form their own association. However, the core purpose remains the same as it was back then which is to help and support former players in need. We have the Old Stars football team, golf days and social events throughout the year which bring together the former players and their families.

Aston Villa FC also play a massive part by supporting the association since we launched, initially through Doug Ellis and now through Randy Lerner, who have been absolutely fantastic with their backing.

Neil Rioch, former Villa defender, 1969–75.
Neil is Chairman of the Aston Villa Former Players Association.
www.astonvillafpa.org

Gerry Hitchens was born in Cannock but was raised in a small mining community in Shropshire and was signed by his boyhood club, Aston Villa in December of 1957 by Eric Houghton from Cardiff City for £20,000. While at Villa, Gerry slowly established himself as questionably, Villa's first iconic striker scoring goals for fun and to this day, still holds the club's post-war goalscoring ratio record. Here, Marcus Hitchens, Gerry's eldest son, talks about a particular memory he has of visiting Villa Park with his late mother, Meriel Hitchens, Gerry's widow.

A particularly memorable day for me was 18 April 1993. I brought my dear mother to Villa Park on the 10th Anniversary of my father, Gerry Hitchens' death. It was a big surprise to mum, although her suspicions were heightened as we turned off at junction six of the M6 motorway!

Marcus Hitchens with Eric Houghton, Meriel Hitchens and Jimmy Dugdale and his wife on 18th April 1993 (10 years after Gerry's death).

The club and I had prepared a two page article in the Aston Villa *News & Record* match-day programme, recalling the 'Memory Match' of 3 December 1960 at Villa Park when Villa beat Manchester City 5–1. On that day, Wylie, O'Neill and McParland bagged one each and dad scored the other two goals. Incidentally a 20-year-old Dennis Law scored the only City goal.

In March 1960, Law signed for Manchester City from Huddersfield Town for what was then a British record transfer fee of £55,000, although Law's share of the fee was reportedly 'precisely nothing'. Once again, Matt Busby had attempted to sign Law for Manchester United, but United's cross city rivals beat them to Law's signature. However, six months later Law was in Italy with Torino and dad would soon to follow him when he left his beloved Villa and signed for Inter Milan in June 1961 for £85,000!

Also in the programme were several photos including one of dad with the great Pelé taken in Cagliari, Sardinia, when the famous Santos team of Brazil were on tour. Dad had last met Pelé in the World Cup Finals in Chile in 1962, although Pelé was injured for the quarter-final tie against England and didn't play. Incidentally, dad scored the only England goal in that match. I also remember there were also recollections of dad from one of his Villa teammates, Vic Crowe, who sadly passed away not so long ago.

After the game, mum enjoyed VIP treatment from the club and met the then manager, 'Big Ron' Atkinson and the team, including the one and only Paul McGrath, Dean Saunders, Mark Bosnich, Tony Daley and Steve Staunton. There was also an emotional reunion with Eric Houghton, who had signed dad from Cardiff in 1957 and we also met up with one of dad's team mates, Jimmy Dugdale and his dear wife. If that wasn't enough for mum to take in, violinist and Villa fanatic, Nigel Kennedy was also around so that was a pleasant bonus and an honour meeting him, as he was at the height of his powers at the time.

Lastly but most definitely not least, this was the first time I was to meet the late and very dear David Goodyear, father of Simon Goodyear (the author of this book). It was a special pleasure to meet him, as he excitedly recounted his fond memories of watching dad as a young man and the great sense of anticipation he had every time he touched the ball.

David, who was the club historian and archivist at the time, as well as a part-time match-day steward, very kindly archived a huge box of newspaper cuttings for me and before you could utter the words, 'From Mine to Milan' he had arranged them all in chronological order in three big files and we arranged to meet so I could pick them up from David's house. My family and I look through them frequently to this day. Not only that, David and I arranged a montage of action and portrait photos of dad, which were eventually mounted in one of the lounges in the North Stand for many years.

It was around this time that David first hinted to me that Gerry's life would make a very good read and that he would be interested in writing his biography. Unfortunately, due to a job move on my part, contact with David lessened through the years, although we exchanged the occasional phone call.

Then, totally out of the blue, in October 2008, I was at home, still quite ill but recovering from a major operation, when the phone rang. The call was from Simon, David's son. Simon had managed to track us down to inform us that David had sadly passed away. Simon had actually rang to say that he had found one of dad's England shirts in a carrier bag and some family photos which I had left with David about 15 years previously. Although the news was very sad, Simon and I spoke at length until he plucked up enough courage to say to me, 'Marcus, how about I write a book about your dad and call it, *The Gerry Hitchens Story?*' To that, I replied those immortal words, 'Have you ever written a book before??' The answer was of course 'no' but what did that matter?

The title of that book was of course, *From Mine To Milan*, and as the saying goes, 'the rest is history'.

Marcus Hitchens, Carmel, Flintshire, North Wales.

This next story touched my heart, as I think it will touch everyone's heart. Simon Fox was born in 1969 to all intents and purposes, a normal, healthy baby boy and born into a family of strong Villa fans. At 13 months he became unwell and was diagnosed with serious heart conditions.

On 18 November 1976, Simon was treated to the time of his life when he was invited to Bodymoor Heath by Ron Saunders to meet him and some of the players. Simon's father, Peter tells the story of his son's 'most memorable day'.

Being from a family of mad Villa fans, one of my relatives got in touch with Ron Saunders and explained the situation about Simon and after a few days Ron duly invited me and Simon to Bodymoor Heath for the day. I hadn't got a car at the time so we had to use public transport. As you can imagine, getting to Bodymoor Heath by bus back then was an ordeal. To make matters worse, we were put on the wrong bus and we had to endure a long walk from somewhere in the middle of the country to the training ground at Bodymoor Heath, carrying Simon for part of the way as he was unwell.

When we finally got there we met Ron Saunders and all the players and they made a real fuss of Simon. Ron made us feel very welcome and we took loads of photos of Simon with the manager and some of the players, including Andy Gray, Chris Nicholl and John Gidman. Simon had the time of his life as he really loved Aston Villa and as his dad, I was really proud of him. He never complained about anything and just got on with it, even though he was very ill.

At the end of the session, we left Ron and the players and started to walk back to the bus stop. After we had been walking for about half an hour, a car passed us, stopped and then reversed back towards us. I said to Simon, 'I hope this isn't someone asking for directions because I haven't got a clue where we are.' As it turned out, it was the Villa skipper, Chris Nicholl. He asked me what I was doing and I told him we were walking to catch the bus. He immediately asked us if we wanted a lift and we obliged and got into his car and he drove us both back into Birmingham city centre. Were we both pleased? Simon just couldn't get over it, having just spent a dream day with his heroes and here he was in the car of the Villa captain Chris Nicholl. What a way to end a fantastic day. It was a moment that will stay with me forever.

The next day, he went to school and told all his mates and he was the envy of the school for weeks to come.

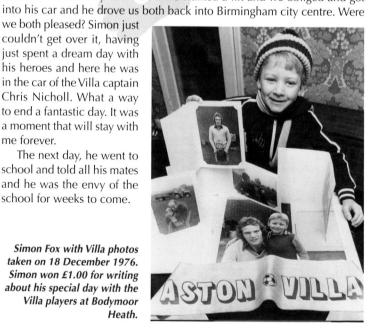

Simon Fox with Villa photos taken on 18 December 1976. Simon won £1.00 for writing about his special day with the Villa players at Bodymoor Heath.

To cap it all, Simon wrote to the *Birmingham Evening Mail* 'Chipper Club' about his 'most memorable day' and his article appeared in the *Mail* on the 21st December 1976, together with a picture of him showing off his photos taken at Bodymoor Heath.

In the last two years of his life I was lucky enough to take Simon to Wembley for the 1977 League Cup Final against Everton. Sadly, we lost Simon after his third operation on 4 July 1978.

As a footnote, I am now a season ticket holder with my grandson, who is also called Simon, named after our son. After we went to Wembley in 2010 for the League Cup Final, my thoughts were about how many father's get to see their football teams play at Wembley with, first their son and in later years, with their grandson.

Peter Fox, Stechford, Birmingham.

Chris Nicholl established himself as a centre-half with Villa between 1972 and 1977. He captained the side to victory over Everton in the 1977 League Cup after two Final replays. The second replay is remembered for Chris scoring one of the greatest goals in any Villa match, a 40-yard left-footer which helped take the match to extra-time. Chris is now the manager of the Aston Villa Old Stars.

We had a training session on a Friday morning and we were due to play Burnley the next day. Ron Saunders got us to practice defending near post corners in this session. We got set up with John Burridge in goal and Keith

Chris Nicholl with Simon Fox at Bodymoor Heath on 18 November 1976.

Leonard in front of me (I'm marking Keith on the near post). Ray Graydon fires the corner into the near post and I go up to head it but 'Budgey' jumps up behind me, smashes his fists towards the ball but instead of punching the ball, hits the back of my head and then I bang my head into the back of Keith Leonard's head.

I was so concussed I couldn't play in the Burnley game. I had to have six stitches in my left eye as my eye was all closed up and I couldn't see out of it. For three months after that incident, the whole of the left side of my head was numb. My eye was closed all that time but as soon as it opened again I got playing again. Since then, I was frightened to death every time the manager asked us to practice defending set pieces. Because of that incident, I have been slightly brain damaged and can't remember much.

I can hardly remember a thing about the matches I played in. Sometime ago a German lad wrote to me telling me about the four goals I scored at Leicester in March 1976. He put in his letter a description of all four goals I scored (two for Villa and two for Leicester). I can only really remember one. I always said that John Burridge was easy to beat and I proved it that day. It was the third goal, and the best goal I vaguely remember. It was a diving header at the far post and I was 6ft in the air, horizontal and flying through the air and the ball passed 'Budgey' and flew into our own top corner. Luckily enough I went onto score at the other end to tie the game at 2–2. After the game, I went to collect the match ball (after 'scoring' four goals) from the referee. It was something I always wanted to do because every time I went to Ray Graydon's house, he'd have five match balls resting on plinths on his mantlepiece, with little notices stating where he collected the match ball from. He'd talk me through every game. So, when I got these four goals against Leicester, I thought to myself, 'Ahr, I'm going to get the ball and put it on a plinth and sit it on my own mantlepiece.' So I went into see the referee but he refused to give me the match ball because he said it was his last game as a referee and he wanted it. So, I never got my ball put on a plinth.

Another time I remember John Gidman, before the 1977 League Cup Final (second replay) had a groin strain. We had about 10 players in his hotel bedroom at the time, and I remember the doctor coming into the room with the biggest syringe I have ever seen. John was naked on the bed and he wouldn't sit still so all the players came in to hold him down while the doctor tried to put this syringe into John. There were three or four players on each arm, and the same on each leg holding him down and the doctor still couldn't get the needle in. It was really funny. Eventually, the doctor got the syringe in and John managed to play for an hour (before the painkiller wore off) in that Final at Old Trafford.

After I'd scored to make it 1–1 in the Final and with about six minutes of normal time to go before the tie went into extra-time, I was on the half way line and I remember some of the lads jumping on me. Leighton Phillips jumps on me and puts his foot right into my eye and my contact lens fell out. When everyone ran to kick-off again, I spent the next minute and a half scouring Old Trafford for my contact lens. I couldn't find it and I had to play the rest of the game with one contact lens, but it didn't affect my timing as my timing was always rubbish anyway.

After the final whistle and we'd won the Cup, I remember coming back out onto the muddy pitch to look for it again. In those days, contact lenses were quite valuable and pricey so it was a big deal to lose one. I still couldn't find it!

However we did it, we won the trophy and to win it at Old Trafford, where we did not win many, it was extra special, even though I did lose a contact lens.

Chris Nicholl, former Villa centre-back, 1972–77.

Nigel Kennedy is probably the best and most well known male violin virtuoso in the world. He made his early career in the classical field, and he has performed and recorded most of the major violin concerti and has more recently included jazz and other genres to his repertoire.

Nigel's recording of Vivaldi's The Four Seasons with the English Chamber Orchestra in 1989 sold over 2 million copies and earned him a place as one of the best-selling classical works ever. The album remained top of the UK classical charts for over a year with sales equivalent to one copy sold every 30 seconds.

Although born in Brighton, Nigel is claret and blue through and through and wowed fans in 2008 when he offered all season card holders free tickets for any date on his 'A Very Nice Album' tour. Being a mad keen Villa fan, he even once painted his Jaguar car in the colours of claret and blue.

Aston Villa have always been and always will be representative of what is good about football. The achievements of our club – from the double-winning team of the late 19th century, through to winning the FA Cup in 1957 for the seventh time; from the League and European Cup winning sides of 1981 and 1982 to our being on the verge of breaking into the top four in the Premier League – have always been matched by an atmosphere and warmth from the most important people at the club – you the fans.

Without the intelligence and inventiveness of our own William McGregor, football would not be the game that people know and love. Before McGregor invented the League format, knock-out competitions like the FA Cup were the only competitions in existence – not just in football but in all sports. Nowadays, and for more than the last hundred years, all team sports use a League format and most of them are completely unaware of their debt to Aston Villa FC when counting up their points tally.

Also, the regal colours of Aston Villa have been borrowed and assumed by other people; not enough West Ham fans care to remember that they

Nigel Kennedy playing his beloved violin in a concert sporting his Villa shirt.

play in claret and blue purely and simply because they literally had to borrow our shirts, before realising that to achieve greatness or something approaching it they would have to continue wearing our colours.

Managers who have made my times watching the club such a priceless and unique experience have included Tommy Docherty, Vic Crowe, Ron Saunders, Tony Barton, Ron Atkinson and Martin O'Neill. Players who have given me memorable experiences on the Holte End include Willie Anderson, John Dunn, Andy Lochhead, Pat McMahon, Brian Godfrey, Jim Cumbes, Bruce Rioch, Chico Hamilton, Ray Graydon, Alex Cropley, John Gidman, Sid Cowans, Tony Morley, Des Bremner, Denis Mortimer, Nigel Spink, Kenny Swain, Gary Shaw, Allan Evans, Ken McNaught, Dean Saunders, Gareth Southgate, Paul McGrath, Tony Daley and Shaun Teale.

More recently, I've loved watching Jaun Pablo Angel, Gabby Agbonlahor, Ashley Young, Richard Dunne, James Collins, Stiliyan Petrov and any other player who hasn't left immediately when he sees more money on another table.

Nigel Kennedy.

Former Birmingham Mail correspondent, Rob Bishop, who is now the *Aston Villa News & Record* programme editor, recalls some magic moments while following Villa.

'I was going to buy Collymore; now I'm going to buy cauliflower!' Ron Atkinson once said in an interview. Even in his darkest moment as Villa manager, Ron Atkinson was still the master of the one-liner. It was the day after Villa had surrendered a 3–1 lead against Wimbledon at Selhurst Park to leave themselves in deep trouble near the foot of the table.

Big Ron had been sacked, yet he still managed an original sign-off quip when asked in a TV interview what he intended to do next. There was an element of truth to his witty reply, too. He genuinely had been looking at Stan Collymore, then with Nottingham Forest, as the answer to a depressing run which had yielded just one Premiership point from nine games.

In the event, Ron's successor Brian Little signed 'Stan the Man' from Liverpool for a club record £7 million two-and-a-half years later, and it didn't work out as successfully as we had hoped. But Ron no doubt reflected for some time after his departure about how things might have turned out differently if he had taken the plunge in 1994 and signed Collymore, who was scoring for fun for Forest while Villa were struggling.

As it was, Atkinson's sacking brought the curtain down on one of the most colourful episodes in Villa's post-war history. Never before had the claret and blue faithful greeted a managerial appointment with the euphoria which accompanied Ron's arrival from Sheffield Wednesday in June 1991. It was such big news that the *Birmingham Mail* produced a 32-page special edition called 'Welcome Back Big Ron' to mark the return of a man who had been on Villa's books as a youngster.

I will never forget the Friday before the opening day of the 1991–92 season, when Villa were due to visit Sheffield Wednesday. Throughout the week there had been stories of Ron needing police protection at Hillsborough, such was the vitriol generated by his summer move from South Yorkshire to Villa Park. Yet on the day of the manager's press conference at Bodymoor Heath, none of us felt brave enough to bring up the subject with Big Ron, who seemed far from his usual bubbly self.

After nearly 10 minutes of tame questions, the room suddenly fell silent. Then Ray Matts, the *Daily Mail* Midlands football correspondent casually leaning against a filing cabinet, uttered the words which had us all – including Atkinson – in fits of laughter. 'If you don't mind me saying so, Ron' he remarked. 'You look like a worried man to me!' I can't think of anyone else who could have delivered that line.

A month or so after Ron's arrival from Hillsborough, Villa headed to Germany on a pre-season tour in July 1991 and I accompanied them on behalf of the *Birmingham Mail*, along with five national reporters, including my old mate, Ray Matts. He was a man of many qualities. A fine journalist, he could always be relied upon to deliver – whether it was a story for his newspaper or a favour for a friend. He had booked a hire car which he collected on landing at Dusseldorf airport. I made the three-hour journey to Hanover with him while our four colleagues – David Harrison, David Moore, John Wragg and Ralph Ellis – travelled in another vehicle. We reached our hotel well ahead of our fellow scribes and Ray treated me to dinner in a nearby restaurant.

Ray was also hugely popular with the players, who knew him as a man to be trusted. He was particularly close to the Villa lads during the 1970s and 1980s – to the extent that they threw him fully-clothed into the bath at Old Trafford following the famous 1977 League Cup Final triumph over Everton. A close friend of Ron Atkinson, he also revealed he had put a good word in for me with Villa's newly-appointed manager, who had asked him for the low-down on the local press corps. As the *Birmingham Mail*'s Villa man, I was going to be dealing with Ron on a regular basis for the foreseeable future so that meant a lot – but Ray's generosity didn't end there.

When he and the other national guys were 'ordered' to Italy the following day to cover David Platt's impending transfer to Bari, I was left on my own in Hanover with a hire car I inherited from Ray. This was all very well, but the team were staying in a country hotel 18 miles away. To ensure I was able to visit the Villa lads every day, Ray told me to use his VW Golf for the duration of my stay.

Having faced the host club and Polish side Gornik in the Hanover Tournament, Villa's third match was against a non-league team near Bremen, a couple of hours' drive away. My intention had been to travel to the match in my hire car, but Big Ron had other plans for me. Paul Mortimer, Villa's new signing from Charlton, was due to join the team on Sunday morning, so Ron asked me to meet the new boy at the airport and take him to Villa's hotel. In return, he said, I could travel on the team coach to the match. Little did I expect to watch the game alongside the boss, the two of us viewing the action from a raised platform at a height of about six feet while Villa's coaching staff and substitutes stood below us on the touchline. I nearly fell off the platform laughing when Ron, having snapped instructions throughout the game, delivered a real gem towards the end of the game. He had been giving full-back Kevin Gage and Danish central defender Kent Nielsen a particularly hard time, and suddenly yelled: 'Gagey! Nielsen! Last 10 minutes. Give it everything you've got.' I pointed out that there were actually only five minutes left, prompting an amended instruction: 'Gagey! Nielsen! Give it twice as much!'

It was during that trip that I discovered Ron has a passion for sporting trivia. He enjoys nothing more than relaxing with a group of like-minded people and firing questions at them. And it simply hates it if you come up with the answer too quickly.

Three years later, Villa played a friendly against one of Ron's former clubs, Atletico Madrid, in the Spanish resort of Ferrol. Secretary Steve Stride and I sat immediately behind Ron during the coach ride from Santiago airport and although the scenery was stunning and the weather glorious, the manager was clearly bored.

Steve and I had been talking about the possibility of Villa Park as a venue for Euro '96 and our conversation was overheard by Ron, who turned and tried to put us on the spot with his latest trivia question.

'Here's one for you,' he said. 'Name all the venues for the 1966 World Cup finals.'

For some unknown reason, the most unlikely one came into my head first. 'Well, there was White City....' 'Forget it,' said Ron indignantly as he turned back to face the front of the coach. 'That's the one I thought you wouldn't get!'

Nigel Spink was not ready when I turned up to interview him at Bodymoor Heath one morning. Villa's goalkeeper was filming with a TV crew on the pitch at the far end of the training ground, so I strolled in that direction to have a chat with him. From a distance, Nigel's imposing frame was clearly identifiable between the goalposts, though I couldn't work out who was taking penalties at him. At a guess, the slightly-built figure was roughly the size of midfielder Adrian Heath, but that assumption was quickly dismissed. The guy took a lengthy run up but barely reached Spink with his weakly-struck penalty. As I drew closer, it suddenly dawned on me that the man on the spot was Nigel Kennedy, the virtuoso violinist who has done more than anyone to popularise classical music. From what I'd just seen, he was not about to give up the day job.

Nigel is Villa's best-known celebrity fan, unless you count Prince William – and this was a long time before Wills decided to adopt the boys in claret and blue as the Royal favourites. Anyway, I can't imagine William taking penalties at the training ground, or Villa's goalkeeper bringing him over to introduce me. 'Sorry I'm late,' said Spink once the filming was over. 'By the way, this is Nigel Kennedy.'

The famous fiddler offered me a huge grin and a robust handshake. 'Hiya monster,' he beamed. 'Hey man, I read all your reports.' Well, I was staggered. Somehow I couldn't picture this musical megastar sitting down and reading what I had to say about Villa. I didn't quite know quite how to respond, so I opted for the cheeky approach: 'Cheers. Your music isn't bad, either!' I was telling the truth, of course. Deep down, it struck me that Nigel was merely being polite. Yet the following December, he proved beyond any question that he really does absorb every snippet of information he can find about his beloved Villa.

Fifteen months after our original meeting, our paths crossed again at a surprise 40th birthday party for Villa secretary Steve Stride and Nigel greeted me like a long-lost pal, eagerly quizzing me about the team's 1–1 draw at Southampton the previous day. It hadn't been too clever, I told him, adding that Villa had been fortunate to leave The Dell with a point after barely creating a worthwhile chance. 'Yes,' he said. 'But you mentioned a couple of incidents in the Argus where they were close to scoring...' I could barely get my head around it. Nigel Kennedy, the nation's best-known classical musician, had ploughed through 40 paragraphs or so of my report on Southampton v Aston Villa in the previous night's *Sports Argus*.

Even more impressive, he'd memorised the key points of the game. But Nigel would really rather watch his team in action than read about them in the press. A longstanding season ticket holder, he only misses home games when he is performing abroad or in a distant corner of Britain.

Nigel, of course, could comfortably afford to watch his favourite team from the luxury of his own executive box, but he's never shown any inclination in that direction. He prefers to soak up the atmosphere from a seat in the stand and he would really be far happier on the terraces, if they still existed. Until Villa Park became an all-seater stadium, he enjoyed nothing more than standing on the Holte End along with thousands of other diehard fans.

Now that's what I call being in tune with your team.

Rob Bishop, *Aston Villa News & Record* programme editor.

Rob is also the co-author of *Aston Villa – The Complete Record* published by DB Publishing.

Dave Ismay is a man of many talents – comedian, entertainer, after dinner speaker, presenter, host, quiz master, MC and actor. He is an experienced, talented and versatile performer, and for over 30 years his skills have taken him to venues all over the world including the entertainment capital itself, Las Vegas (and Villa Park). He loves football in general and Aston Villa in particular. Dave has kindly written exclusively for me about some of his experiences and memories of the Villa.

A former wife once complained, 'You think more of Villa than you do of me.' I retorted, 'Dear heart, I think more of Blues than I do of you.' To follow the Villa is an encapsulation of life itself. You experience every human emotion, sentiment, feeling or passion that life has to offer and too often it seems even within the same game. I do differ however with those who equate the same ecstasy in scoring a goal to that of sexual gratification. That really is a sad analogy! The enigmatic 'claret and blues' can nevertheless take you to unparalleled highs of adrenalin rush to unplumbed depths of unbearable grief and despondency. Nothing is ever mundane and ordinary and from as far back as my fading memory permits my moods have been governed by their results.

As a lad I used to catch the Villa Park special bus from the 'Hall of Memory' in Broad St to the 'Hall of Memory' in Aston as the local joke was regaled by music hall comedians. I mostly stood in the Trinity Rd Stand with the odd excursion, weather forecast permitting, onto the (then) open-topped Holte End.

I owe my Villa allegiance and devotion to a legend in junior football, a one Bert Ewington, my substitute father and a fanatic who was still turning out as a stopper centre-half for Harborne Athletic when in his sixties. He used to tell 'Mick' his long suffering and fretful wife he was only taking his boots in case someone forgot theirs! For the atmospheric night games he and I used to cycle to and from Villa Park and I learned more about life in general and Villa in particular from this absolute gentleman and truly inspirational figure than anyone else in my formative years.

When I met and became pals with Doug Ellis my seating arrangements changed forever. Except for the period when 'Deadly' was ousted by the Bendalls (and that's a book in itself) I have been so fortunate in being allowed to view my obsession from privileged positions in Director's boxes or their equivalent within some of the greatest footballing theatres. I have also been lucky enough to work at the shrine of my worship for nearly 15 years which makes selecting a couple of anecdotes from literally hundreds of candidate a difficult task.

Here then are two stories which are probably just a little different in content and which I hope will entertain you. Both coincidently are from 1983.

In the European Cup (now the Champions League) quarter-final we had drawn Juventus, a wonderful and talented team brimming with internationals and orchestrated by the great Michel Platini. We had lost the home leg 2–1 after putting up a good fight but the return leg looked like a foregone conclusion and so it proved. After a dreadful Jimmy Rimmer slip and a Ken McNaught blunder we were losing badly and three down when Pete Withe grabbed a consolation. I leapt to my feet and angrily, stupidly and unreasonably screamed, 'now let's get three more and bury these cocky b******s'. Deadly looked suitably embarrassed by my crass outburst and was pointedly and rightly asked by his Italian counterpart the literal translation of which was, 'who is the rude loudmouthed idiot?' He never missed a beat, smiled benignly and said, 'Il Presidenti' before tapping the side of his head in the universal accepted gesture that signifies 'barmy.' From then onwards I had little option but to nod and acknowledge all the patronising

Gerry Hitchens (right) with John Charles (left) outside Villa Park prior to the Villa v Juventus European Cup game in March 1983.

handshakes and sympathetic looks from the Italian clubs officials before we were all transferred at great speed to Turin airport, hustled through check-in and herded into transport taking us to the aircraft sitting as a vague speck on the very outskirts of the airports perimeter.

The Italians clearly wanted rid of the invading Brummie hordes as soon as possible without the honour of female members of their families being at risk for another night.

Doug held back from the crowd and after resisting or ignoring all attempts to force him into the final vehicle, gestured to me to join him in a leisurely walk across the tarmac to the plane. It was a surreal moment. The moon was shining, the sky was almost black and the stars were twinkling. We had just been stuffed by one of the world's finest teams and yet our chairman was in philosophical and munificent mood as we strolled across the tarmac. 'Shouldn't we hurry?' I suggested. 'Can they go without me?' He quietly replied. In that five minute walk we talked about all things except football during which I learned this was his method of achieving catharsis. Perhaps in his heart he also knew that this result and its manner were to implement the break-up of the great European Cup-winning team.

That was not the only time I let him and myself down with silly angry outbursts following defeats when a much more restrained and sporting response was required given my surroundings. Inevitably Doug would reprimand me in private but always find some reason to excuse and defend my behaviour in public. So much has been said and written about 'Deadly' over the years, some of it accurate and self-inflicted but most of it manufactured chip wrappings. Maybe one day I'll write the definitive 'Deadly' book. Someone needs to!

In May 1983 I was booked to appear as cabaret in The Royal Swazi Spa Hotel (yes, that's a genuine hotel) in the southern African kingdom of Swaziland. The occasion was a football tournament between the Swazi national side, Spurs and the mighty reds of Manchester United. With the authorities lapsing border restrictions the expectation was for thousands of expats living in South Africa to make the accessible trip to watch their heroes. Manchester United were taken to a Cup Final replay with Brighton which meant they were effectively four days late arriving at the hotel. I remember the double take and disbelieving face of Big Ron Atkinson, their manager and my pal from his days at West Brom, as I welcomed him and the team into the hotel dressed from head to toe in Villa kit, with claret and blue bunting totally engulfing the reception area and my record of 'A.S.T.O.N V.I.L.L.A'. blasting over the tannoy system.

It was a fun week to say the least. Ex-Villa hero John Gidman, still weary from the previous nights partying, fell off the back of the raised first tee in the golf tournament and decided to remain there to sleep it off. We covered him with a mosquito net and left him. A large family sitting down to breakfast was alarmed to find their table moving seemingly of its own violation until the dishevelled figure of Ray Wilkins emerged mumbling his apologies and rubbing the sleep from his eyes.

It was here when I first learned of the power of the name of Aston Villa. For the first game the two English clubs were paired together and had left the hotel sometime earlier. I joined the smaller coach taking the officials and directors of both clubs to the national stadium. Although we had police escorts of kind, plain clothes officers on Vespa scooters, it was hardly surprising we quickly became detached and subsequently stranded in a huge traffic jam with everyone apparently gridlocked. I was also doing some commentary for South African Television so it was imperative I made it to the stadium before kick-off. I opened my window and beckoned imperiously to a huge and massively perspiring, fully yet ill fittingly uniformed policeman, 'Do you know who I am?' I demanded. He shook his head yet had the decency to attempt to appear shamefaced. 'My name is Douglas Ellis. I am the Chairman of Aston Villa and I have an appointment with your Queen.' His reaction was startling as was the faces of the two genuine chairmen in the coach; Douglas Alexiou of Spurs and Martin Edwards of United. He snapped to attention, saluted and immediately began to kick various vehicles surrounding ours shrieking at them 'to move ass or be shot' as I recall. Amazingly as with the Red Sea in biblical times the storm abated the waves parted and somehow we drove through making it in time for the official presentation. For years 'Do you know who I am?' was always the opening gambit when I met either of these footballing luminaries, and even today Martin and I still enjoy a chuckle about it.

The commentary on the games was a fascinating experience, which if nothing else I discovered just how difficult a job Messrs John Motsom, Brian Moore and Ken Wolstenholme actually managed and how effortless they made it seem. Obviously, I would find the pronunciation of the full names of the local team difficult so I was allowed and in fact encouraged to use their tribal names. I remember Roger Big Dogger, Zebra Flyer and Black Happy Cloud and believe I had the temerity to include the following joke concerning the Swazi national manager. 'His wife is called Five Horses' 'What does that mean?' asked my straight man. 'Nag nag nag nag nag!' I replied.

It was in the coffee shop of the hotel in the wee small hours with 'Big Ron' and his staff drinking tea, yes tea and pots of it when the news came though of 'Sid' Cowans scoring for England against Scotland and his proposed move to Napoli was disintegrating. Even in darkest Africa the Villa connections were powerful and provoking, and up until a few years ago had a supporters club based at the wonderfully named 'Why Not' night club-cum-bordello based in its capital Mbabane.

Dave Ismay, all round entertainer and life long Villa fan.

Jimmy Brown was signed from Midlothian boys by Tommy Docherty in 1969 and was part of the team that won the FA Youth Cup in 1972. He holds the club record for being the youngest ever player to appear for Aston Villa at the age of 15 years and 349 days, a record which due to current employment laws could stand forever. Jimmy was also the youngest-ever captain of Villa at the age of 19.

Jimmy talks here about how he signed for Tommy Docherty and his Villa debut.

I nearly didn't sign for Villa. I should have played for Arsenal if I'm honest; in fact I'd agreed to sign for the Gunners in May 1969 but if it was not for Peter Docherty (no relation to the former Villa manager), who was a scout for Villa at the time, I'd have been wearing the red and white of Arsenal not the claret and blue of Villa. Peter had been watching me for some time and tracked me down to my parents' home in Edinburgh just after I had played for Scotland schoolboys in the Victory Shield. I had already looked at a number of other clubs including Rangers and Celtic but I liked the look and feel of Arsenal. When we met, Peter was ok with me looking at other clubs and setting my sights on playing for Arsenal but he just wanted me to come down to Birmingham for a few days and have a look around Villa Park. So, I went with my parents and the club put us up at the Albany Hotel for the weekend and we were offered days out at the horse racing and such like. I trained with the first team and got involved with a practise match and I actually enjoyed it and I thought it all went really well.

When I first met Tommy (Docherty), he was adamant I was going to sign for him. 'So, you gonna sign for us then? We want you here.' When I told him I had agreed terms with Arsenal, Tommy was furious and said, 'Arsenal, f***ing Arsenal!!! I'm not having that!!! I'll have a word with Peter about that.' I assumed by that reaction, Peter hadn't told him. He then took me and my parents into the office where I met Doug Ellis for the first time. Tommy pointed to a chair and said, 'Jim, you sit there,' while he led my dad into another office for a chat. Sometime later, I signed the papers for Villa, a Second Division club!! Arsenal were a top four First Division club. I only intended to train

Jimmy Brown caricature - Aston Villa's youngest player.

50

with Villa and see what it was like but I ended up signing that weekend. My thoughts were that I would stand a better chance to play first-team football at Villa rather than sit in the reserves at Arsenal for a few years.

I made my Villa debut on 17 September 1969 away to Bolton Wonderers. It was an evening match and I distinctly remember seeing their classy centre-back, Charlie Hurley lining up before the kick-off. He must have been in his 40s and nearing retirement. He looked like the Hagrid character from Harry Potter; he was a giant of a man and a player who was nick-named, 'The King' and I was this 15-year-old, petite, wafer-thin, long-haired, schoolboy lining up against him. I looked over at him, and he looked back and gave me an unfriendly wink. I looked around the pitch at the other players and I thought to myself some of these guys looked quite 'old' compared to me. I say 'old,' most of them were late 20s. I had been used to playing with kids in the youth team and I didn't really know anything about playing against men. I was terrified! We lost that game.

The next week I made my home debut against Hull City and we beat them 3–2. We were losing 2–0 early on and I thought, 'Oh, no!! We won't come back from that.'

I liked Tommy. He was a great motivator; great if you were one of 'his' players, but if you weren't he would try and get rid of you if you weren't what he wanted. At times he could be quite cynical and frightening. I remember we played Manchester United at Old Trafford and we lost 2–1. After the game, Tommy said to me that I was going to be sold to United. He was not happy with my performance. I was shocked at his statement. A few weeks later, I was still at Villa and I asked him what that was all about me going to United and he told me I was staying. Tommy could blow hot and cold sometimes.

Although I was signed by Tommy Docherty it was Vic Crowe who made me captain in the 1972–73 season when we finished third in the Second Division. However, in those days, it was two up, two down so we missed out on promotion.
Jimmy Brown, former Villa midfielder, 1969–75.

As a young lad growing up in Witton and Perry Barr and an avid Villa fan my hero was Gerry Hitchens. I was always so excited when a football magazine had his picture in or I was lucky enough to get his card from a tea packet! Unfortunately he had stopped playing for Villa by the time I was allowed to attend matches at the age of 14 so I never saw him play, something I have regretted over the years. I felt sick in the stomach when I learnt of his untimely death. Gerry and his like were true heroes in the strictest sense of the word, not like the overpaid primadonnas and mercenaries of today.
Ron Watkins, Sissinghurst, Kent.

Throughout all my adult years of supporting Villa my pre-match activity has been largely the same, whether home or away. Start out early; arrive at the ground in good time; meet up with friends and relatives; have a drink and a meal then into the ground for team news and pre-match build up. I hate missing kick-off but over the years there have been a couple of occasions when my pre-match routine has not gone according to plan.

One such time was on Saturday 13 September 1969. Two years earlier Villa had been relegated from the top flight but with a boardroom revolution led by Doug Ellis, Tommy Docherty installed as manager and a big pre-season spending spree, prospects looked good for the 1969–70 season; speculation wasn't so much as to whether Villa would win the old Second Division, rather by how many points they would finish ahead of their nearest rivals. However, the season hadn't started as expected. The opening day home defeat against Norwich City was a shock, but the first seven games brought only two points, from draws at Carlisle United and at home to Millwall. In addition, the club had been knocked out of the Football League Cup in the second round by West Bromwich Albion at Villa Park.

The next game was at newly promoted Watford, a club that had never previously played higher than the old Third Division. Watford were looking for their first win having also gained just two points, with two draws, the Hornets sat at the bottom of the table on goal average (the system in force at the time) with Villa a place above. Surely we could look forward to the first victory of the season. Docherty made a number of changes to the side. John Dunn, who had been on the transfer list until the previous week and who had not played since the opening day defeat was reinstalled in goal, with Evan Williams stepping down. Full-back Charlie Aitken was left out with young Brian Rowan making his Villa debut and having to face Watford's star winger, Stewart Scullion. There was no place for 'Chico' Hamilton or Mike Ferguson, while 19-year-old John Griffiths was named as substitute.

I had arranged to go to Watford with my brother, Roy, who had travelled to all Villa's games home and away during the painful descent down the top-flight table and continuing in the Second Division. However Roy had to work on the morning of the game. No problem, I thought, it would just be a matter of collecting him from McKechnie Brothers in Aldridge, where he worked, and we would drive down to Watford. In those days the M1 didn't stretch as far as it now does now and traffic was heavy as we inched our way through Birmingham. Having reached the motorway, the traffic was even worse, it was a slow crawl all the way and we arrived in Watford after kick-off, hastily parking the car. It was Villa's first ever visit to Watford for a competitive game and we were mistaken for West Ham fans by some locals who obviously were not aware that the colours we were wearing were the same as the Hammers. They decided to 'take us on.' We were more intent on getting into the ground and it must have seemed a strange sight as we ran down the road immediately followed by the chasing pack.

Fifteen minutes play had elapsed when we entered the ground, and after running up the bank at the back of the terracing we emerged just in time to see Villa skipper, Brian Tiler, hit an awkward bouncing ball into the back of the net. I was three foot in the air cheering when two thoughts hit me simultaneously: one, I was unaware that Villa 'keeper John Dunn had been transferred to the Hornets and two, why were the Villa fans not celebrating?

I came back to earth realizing the truth which was almost too painful to comprehend: Tiler had scored in his own net!

Unfortunately if this was bad, the rest of the game was even worse, although Villa somehow managed to survive until the break with just the one goal deficit. It couldn't last and two minutes into the second half the home side doubled their advantage when Tom Walley ran on to a free kick 25 yards out and drove the ball through Villa's defensive wall before Dunn could move. Docherty immediately withdrew Pat McMahon from the attack and replaced him the inexperienced John Griffiths. John Dunn was having a nightmare in goal, although he did well to save when Colin Franks was clean through. Meanwhile Villa were unable to make any impact in attack, a solitary shot from Bruce Rioch presenting the only danger with Griffiths, who had taken up the centre-forward position, finding it difficult to have any impact on the game. As the match wore on it became increasingly dominated by Watford and a third goal followed from a terrible mistake by Dunn. Hornets full-back Duncan Welbourne took a free kick five yards inside the Villa half which he touched to Keith Eddy. The midfielder floated the ball into the Villa goalmouth. Unfortunately the goalkeeper had come too far out and the ball floated over his head and into the net. Watford had gained their first ever Second Division win and Villa, boasting the most expensive side in the division, plunged to the foot of the table. It was the only Villa game for Rowan and the last of Griffiths' three appearances, two as substitute.

These were indeed desperate days. One correspondent to the Birmingham Mail even appealed to supporters to provide loans so that Mr Docherty could buy a couple more players. However, it was not all glum news; the same paper reported that a Villa supporting Irishman had moved from his home country to live in Aston so as to be near his beloved club. In addition, Docherty's wholesale team changes had resulted in Villa reserves gaining their first Central League win of the season.

Docherty lasted until the following January, when with the team rooted to the foot of the table and out of the FA Cup, he was sacked following a 5–3 home defeat by Portsmouth. Doc's assistant Vic Crowe took over the helm and pulled the club round but, despite a gallant effort, at the end of the season the team were relegated to the third tier. In three short years the club had plunged from the top tier to the Third Division. However, even this has to be put into perspective, my brother Roy was later to die suddenly, aged 48 years. Sometimes there are more important things than football.

It was almost eight years later when I next arrived late for a match. The turmoil of '69 was long-since forgotten. Vic Crowe had steered Villa to two glorious seasons in the Third Division during which there was a magnificent League Cup semi-final victory over Manchester United when Pat McMahon, the player the Doc took off at Watford, scored the winner in a 2–1 second leg victory to take Villa to Wembley. The Third Division Championship was won with a record points haul. Unfortunately Crowe was not able to take the club to the next step. Ron Saunders took over in 1974 and steered Villa back to the top flight and a League Cup Final win against Norwich City in his first season at the helm.

On 22 February 1977 I was on a Travellers Club coach to Arsenal for a League Cup semi-final replay against Queen's Park Rangers after the first leg at Loftus Road had finished goalless and a double from John Deehan had given Villa a 2–2 draw at Villa Park. We were roughly half way down the M1 when the coach suddenly came to a standstill. There were obvious mechanical problems. It is difficult to imagine now, in the age of mobile 'phones and easy communications, the anguish this caused; there was no such technology at the time. Firstly the driver had to walk down the hard-shoulder of the motorway to locate a telephone point. Having 'phoned his depot he returned with the news that either a replacement coach would be sent from Birmingham or arrangements would be made for a local firm to send transport to our rescue. We then had to endure a very long wait, not knowing of any further developments. Eventually the driver of a coach travelling in the opposite direction flashed the lights, a signal we took to mean that this might be our replacement coach. We then had to endure a further anxious wait before the coach re-appeared on our side of the motorway. It was indeed our replacement transport. However, the joy of this was short-lived. We were told that our original driver would have to remain with the broken-down vehicle and the replacement coach driver explained that he could not take us to Arsenal and back as he was already close to his permitted driving hours, having worked during the day. The best he could do was to drive us to his depot in Luton and enquiries would then be made in an effort to locate a fresh driver who was willing and able to do the job.

Our relief at arriving at the coach depot in Luton was tempered by the knowledge that time was fast ticking by. I had not missed a game at home or away during the decade and this record seemed to be in serious jeopardy, particularly when the extent of the problem was explained. Because the coach would have to return to the Luton depot that night after taking us to Highbury and then back to Birmingham, they would have to find a driver who had not worked at all during that day and who was willing to come in at very short notice and work until the early hours of the following morning. Kick-off time was fast approaching and we were stuck in Luton, but eventually a driver arrived and we were on our way. We stood no chance of making kick-off but we just might make the second-half. This, however, was the turning point. Traffic from then on into London was kind to us, the early evening rush having finished and, as we approached Highbury, the roads were completely clear around the ground, with the match already well in progress.

We arrived 20 minutes after kick-off and dashed into the ground. We then had to run up several flights of stairs to the top of Highbury. I emerged into the floodlit stadium completely out of breath and immediately gazed straight down onto the pitch below just in time to see Dennis Mortimer slot the ball through to Brian Little who went past QPR 'keeper Phil Parkes to score. This time I was three foot in the air and there was no nasty surprise. Villa 'keeper John Burridge was at the other end of the pitch celebrating, it really was the QPR goalkeeper that Brian Little had beaten. Seven minutes later Little doubled the advantage when Alex Cropley took a corner, Parkes fisted the ball out and the striker made no mistake, neatly slotting the ball home from 12 yards.

After the break, QPR fought hard to get back into the game but with Chris Nicholl and Leighton Phillips resolute in defence and Dennis Mortimer controlling the midfield plus Andy Gray and John Deehan up front; it was a formidable task for Rangers. There were however, one or two scares before Mortimer broke on the left in the 89th minute and centered for Little to ram the ball home with Parkes stranded to complete his hat-trick. Villa had reached a record fifth League Cup Final in style and would go on to take the trophy after an epic three-match Final against Everton when Little would provide a win with two goals.

Manager Ron Saunders steered the club to the League title in 1981 and the following year Villa were crowned champions of Europe. The dark days of 1969 became just a distant memory, but I still always make sure I am not late for the game....just in case!

Frank Holt, Tamworth, Staffordshire.
Frank is the co-author of *Aston Villa – The Complete Record*, published by DB Publishing.

Being from a family full of mainly Bluenoses, I'm claret and blue through and through. My dad wouldn't take me down the Blues so my uncle Roy took me down the Villa – you go once, you go for life; I'm now on my 53rd year as a Villa fan. My mother, father, three brothers and two sisters are all Birmingham and Celtic fans; I'm a Villa and a Rangers fan. The simple reason for being a Rangers fan is my Uncle Bob took me to see Rangers play one year and I saw a player called Jim Baxter, who was a very good player. Rangers had the same badge as Villa as well (in the 1960s) and I've followed them ever since. I just love Aston Villa Football Club. I've met some unbelieveable people and made some fantastic friends with my association with Villa.

I don't tend to 'boo' Villa players; it's no good to the club or player; however, I have only booed two players and they both deserved it in my opinion. Steve Hodge because he wanted away and because he gave the ball away during the Norwich game and led to a goal. The other one was Nigel Callaghan, who seemed to stand in the middle of the park and if the ball wasn't at his feet he had the attitude, 'why should I run for it?' I look at some of the players who have played for Villa in the past who fight for the club; the likes of Des Bremner, who still runs his heart out playing for the Villa Old Stars. He destroyed Paul Brietner in the European Cup Final, who was a major player for Bayern at the time. Another one I can name is Paul Birch, not graced with great skill but he played with heart and passion and he was special like that. I love 'workers' in football. You can have all the skill in the world but if you can't be bothered when it's cold you don't perform, that's why I love the 'workers.' My favourite Villa player of all time has got to be Paul MacGrath. There's only one word to describe him in my opinion and that's "phenomenal!"

Talking about skill, in my time we've never had a centre-forward with natural skill until the arrival of Savo. We've had the lionhearts like Withe and Gray but Savo had the skill to go with it. He did get ridiculed and his big mistake was he said, 'I'm going to do (this and that)...' In my opinion you shouldn't say you are going to do something until you've done it. The other big mistake he made was spitting at Blackburn.

One game which sticks out in my memory of watching Villa is when we beat Blues 5–1 at Villa Park in 2008. It was unbelievable. For a Villa fan to see that display and to see the Blues supporters leaving the ground at half-time it was a great feeling.

I've seen League Cup wins and what have you and went to the European Cup Final. I travelled to Rotterdam without a passport. I went on a day trip visa but ended up spending a week in Holland – that's a long story. I went to British Rail and bought this blue card which was stamped in a sort of braille. The rest of the lads were going for a week and I managed to get out of the country and stayed with the lads for a week. I was only meant to go the day of the game. To go and watch my team be crowned 'Kings of Europe', that team from B6 – 'Kings of Europe' was special!!

There are so many games I can recall. When we won the League at Highbury – we spent nearly a week in London. We got there on the Thursday and came back on the Tuesday night and went to watch Villa play Birmingham in a friendly – it may have been Joe Gallagher's testimonial or something. Just to see them win one major trophy is worth supporting that team but doing what we done in those three years was special.

I remember my Grandad taking me to see the '57 lads bring back the FA Cup in an open-top bus around Birmingham. To see the current Villa team do that would be the one thing I'd love to see in my life time. I just love seeing Villa play – that's how my life is.

John Ross (brother of BRMB presenter, Tom Ross), Tile Cross, Birmingham.

I was actually born at 3pm just as Villa were kicking off in a game in 1921. It was the only match my father missed I think. I was brought up with stories of players like Billy Walker and the great 'Pongo' Waring. So, how could I not become a Villa supporter? However, I must have been in the minority as very few women went to football games back then. One of the best memories I have was during the 1936–37 season and I was down the Villa with my father. Jimmy Allen was captain back then and in this particular game, which I can't remember who it was against, he was having a rotten game and everyone was completely fed up of him. With the crowd in almost silence, all of a sudden a voice shouts out, 'Hey Allen, why don't you abdicate?' This match must have been just after the abdication of King Edward VIII in December 1936.

Another match I remember was the FA Cup semi-final played at Bramall Lane against Preston and dad and I went up on the train. The fans' favourites in those days were Frank Broome and Frank Shell so some of the supporters got off the train at Sheffield carrying brooms over their shoulders and some were carrying trays (the kind Ushers use in cinemas to carry ice creams) full of seaside shells. In those days it was funny. Today, you wouldn't be allowed in the ground carrying a broom!

My late husband was also a Villa supporter and it was through the Villa (indirectly) that we first spoke to each other. I was on the bus coming home from work one day wearing a claret and blue top and this man came to sit next to me. He said, 'You're a Villa supporter aren't you?' I said I was and the rest is history, as they say.

Betty Sheward, Bournville, Birmingham.

Frank Broome played for Villa 1934–47.

The first game for which I ever queued up for tickets was when I was 14 years old. I got there at 10 o'clock on the Sunday morning they went on sale. The queue was huge and the back of the queue was about 50yds from the Holte pub and heading down Witton Lane! It was three or four wide right down to Witton Island, round the corner, through the side streets and back onto Trinity Road, then along to the old ticket office. I didn't think I stood a chance at getting a ticket, but if I recall correctly, I got my tickets about two in the afternoon, as did the hundred or so that joined the queue after me. Happy Days!

Ken Baldwin, Lichfield, Staffordshire.

My father was a life long supporter of Aston Villa so after World War Two when I was about 11 years old, he said to me, 'You've got to come down the Villa.' So I had to go and from that day on I was a Villa fan. This was the 1945–46 season and Villa were in the Football League (South). I don't particularly remember the first match I went to; it may have been West Ham but I do remember the second match. It was 2nd February 1946 and Villa played at home to Tottenham Hotspur and they won 5 – 1. Villa still had a lot of pre-war players still playing for them who were getting on a bit but they knew what they were doing on the pitch. I only remember that the fifth goal against Tottenham was a penalty; which was scored by Cummings after he hit the post and scored from the rebound.

We would usually sit in the stand as I was only little then. I began to go regularly by then and I particularly remember 1946–47 being a really bad year for weather during the winter. During one game, it snowed and it snowed and it snowed until during the second half, with the score at 2–2 the referee called the game off. It was the only time I can recall a game being postponed during the game.

During the Christmas of 1947, the Villa goalkeeper, Joe Rutherford had been injured during a game against Wolves at Villa Park. Of course there were no substitutes in those days so subsequently they had to find another 'keeper. I think they had Alan Wakeman but they put Keith Jones in to deputise for Rutherford. Jones was very young, Welsh and totally inexperienced. In the famous FA Cup match on 10 January 1948 against a very strong Manchester United side, Jones was thrown into the fire. In those days, I seem to recall Villa nearly always used to get knocked out in the third round and that year was no exception. However, this was no run-of-the-mill Cup tie. Within 13 seconds, Edwards scored for Villa, virtually straight from the kick off. By half-time, the visitors had put five goals into Jones' net. They ran rings round the Villa defence. I sat in the stand with my father and 58,000 other Villa fans wondering what to expect in the second half. Villa pulled three goals back shortly after the break. How they did it I don't know. The only goal I remember was Dickie Dawsett scoring from the penalty spot. He hit the ball very hard and put the ball in the net to make it 5–4 to United. Unfortunately, United scored again to stop an unthinkable revival. It was just an unforgettable match, even though the score wasn't in our favour.

On New Year's Day 1949, I took my cousin to the Villa to see them play Blackpool. He had never been to a football match before and so I persuaded him to come along. Big mistake!! We lost 5–2 at home and the result took us to the foot of the table. Relegation was looming – Villa couldn't get relegated could they? We'd settle for mid-table but relegation was unthinkable. So, the Board followed up their purchase of Ivor Powell a few weeks before Christmas with the transfer of 'Con' Martin and Colin Gibson. Powell and Martin tightened up the Villa defence so much that they only lost one League game after the Blackpool defeat and they finished mid-table.

In November 1949, Villa played Sunderland at home and our goalkeeper, Keith Jones unfortunately came to grief. In those days, players were allowed to challenge the goalkeeper to the ball. The Sunderland player, I think his name was Davies, shot the ball at Jones and he parried it away but Davies came back for the rebound and challenged Jones for the ball and collided with the Welshman and broke Jones's arm. It was a terrible injury. To everyone's surprise, who should go in goal but 'Con' Martin. There were no substitutes in those days so someone had to go in goal and I believe he had played in goal before. He did ok as Villa won the game 2–0. A couple of seasons later, Martin played in goal for almost half a season for one reason or another. He had good cover, though, in Frank Moss at centre-half. Martin was a big chap and he was a decent 'keeper. I remember in one game the ball came over towards him at his right hand side and he stuck his hand out and picked the ball out of the air with one hand.

In those days, we lived in Hodge Hill, near the Fox & Goose pub and I remember seeing 'Con' Martin there doing his shopping as he was living in one of the rented properties in the area that Villa owned.

Then there was Colin Gibson, a winger they picked up from Newcastle and he cost alot of money as well. Frank Broome, a marvellous player in his day, was sold in 1947 because he was involved in the Players Union and that was not acceptable for the Villa Board. Before buying Gibson, they tried Johnny Dixon on the right wing but that was not his best position, although he performed all right and scored a few goals. I remember his red face and blond hair and him rushing down the right wing with the ball, even though he never seemed to have the ball under any great control. When he came to centring the ball it could have gone anywhere, and usually it did. He wasn't a Stanley Matthews who placed the ball into the centre of the box for the centre-forward to score. Gibson just seemed to kick it into the middle of the box and hoped for the best.

When Villa played Portsmouth in 1952 Gibson was doing his stuff on the wing and kicked this one ball into the middle of the penalty area. By the time the ball reached the middle, it found Dixon, playing as an inside-right, at waist height in front of him. It wasn't the sort of ball that anybody would cope with but Dixon launched himself forward, got his head to the ball and it went straight into the roof of the net in real Dixon style.

Villa have always been short of centre-forwards it seems but another match around that time I went to and Gibson was put in as a striker of all places. His ball control as a striker was equally inefficient and against Middlesbrough he was in the penalty area, facing his own goal and the ball came to him on the ground with Dixon running alongside him. All he had to do was knock the ball back for Dixon to shoot. By the time

Gibson had got the ball under control, it was almost too late as Dixon had gone past him. However, somehow Dixon managed to keep his right foot behind him and got hold of the ball and hit it right into the top corner of the net. Dixon was a wonderful player; a real goal poacher.

Billy 'Cowboy' Goffin was another player I have fond memories of. He did not have great talent but he would have died for the Villa. They said if Goffin bled, the blood would be claret and blue. Goffin played in various positions along the forward line but when they were short of a left winger Goffin would slip into that position because he could actually kick with his left foot, a skill alot of footballers can't perfect. Against Bolton in 1951, the Trotters scored very early in the game and Villa tried and tried to pull one back. They couldn't get an equaliser until 10 minutes from time with the ball out on the right wing and it was knocked across the goal area along the ground when suddenly from nowhere, Goffin popped up to knock the ball into the net. We all went home very relieved that Villa hadn't lost a game we should have won.

At the beginning of the 1951–52 season dad and I went to an away game at Stoke; my only away game as it turned out. The Villa goal, scored by Dixon was something to shout about, even if the final score was not . He picked the ball up from the centre circle and ran straight as an arrow down the pitch, dodging the defenders and planted the ball into the net. It was a marvellous goal but we still lost 4–1.

As hearsay suggested that the Club was run by the Board, the manager would pick the team and if the Board did not agree with his selection, they would change it. Villa had no youth policy but had a reserve side composed of people who were either 'past it' or what were called 'permanent reserves' – players who would come into the team when a first teamer was injured. Such names as Albert Vinall, Larry Canning (later to become a BBC Radio 5 Live broadcaster), Amos Moss (he had a brother called Frank who played for Villa) and Reg Lowe (who also had a brother, called Eddie who played for Villa). However, it was usual for the Board to go out and buy another player (for as little money as they could) if the team was short in a particular position. Some purchases were successful, some were awful. They bought 'Sailor' Brown who was 'over the hill' from Nottingham Forest; I think he was sick on the pitch once. He didn't last long and only spent a season with Villa. Some of the better players they bought in the late 1940s included the likes of Trevor Ford. Just as it is today, players came to the Villa in those days, did their stuff and then they said 'we want to win something....You can't win here. We're off....' Of course, when Sunderland offered £30,000 for Ford in 1950 the Board couldn't resist the money. The same happened with Danny Blanchflower. They bought him from Barnsley as a relatively unknown, but he was a marvellous player. After a few years at Villa he was off to Tottenham where he subsequently had a wonderful career. More recently, Dwight Yorke springs to mind. He was a brilliant player but he wanted to win things.

Stan Lynn was a decent player Villa picked up cheaply from Third Division (North) side Accrington Stanley. He was a very tough player. He had a few games in the reserves at first but then they found that Lynn could kick the football rather hard. I did wonder whether he kicked it with his toe but there was no doubt about it when it came to taking a penalty or a free kick from just outside the area, Stan Lynn was the master. I recall he scored a hat-trick in a game against Sunderland at Villa Park in January 1958 and he scored from the spot and from a free-kick. Then Villa had a corner on the right hand side. Usually, a corner was taken and fired into the middle of the box and everyone jumped up. For some reason, this particular corner was different. Maybe they had worked it out in training but the ball was played along the ground towards the corner of the six-yard box. Lynn came rushing up the park and connected with the ball and it went straight into the top corner. In those days, it was not normal for full-backs to do that. Full backs defended and booted the ball as far as they could and weren't meant to go rushing up field to score hat-tricks. Then there was Peter Aldis who scored the most amazing header from the half way and it was probably his only goal for the club.

One League Cup game I remember was the infamous match against Manchester United in the 1970 semi-final. We stood no chance on paper. United had the likes of Best, Charlton and Law, even though they didn't win anything in those post European Cup days, they were still a First Division side and pretty formidable for a third tier Villa side. There was no earthly chance of Villa doing anything there but at Old Trafford, somehow Villa scraped a 1–1 draw. In the replay at Villa Park, I went to the game and when Kidd scored for United in the first half, we thought that was that. Then, with the ball out on the right touchline it was lofted hopefully into the United penalty area, where stood Andy Lochhead, in front of the United centre-half, who jumped for the ball and it spun off the top of his famous bald head into the back of the United net. I don't think he knew where the ball was going but it was a goal and it kept us in the game. You could cut the air with a knife and the crowd went mad. It was a huge crowd, 62,500 that night. That goal encouraged the Villa when 10 minutes from time, Willie Anderson found himself free on the left wing, centred the ball into the path of McMahon and it was 2–1. The goal put Villa into the Final, where they unfortunately lost to Tottenham.

My wife had an uncle called Jeremiah Griffiths who played for Villa between 1895 and 1897. We knew this because we had a Cup winner's medal which he had won in the 1897 FA Cup Final against Everton (even though he didn't play). We, therefore, had to find something out about the medal and about Jeremiah. He was a half back and played three times for Villa, including an appearance in the semi-final against Liverpool. Although he didn't play in the Final, the club gave him a medal. We eventually auctioned the medal a few years ago.

Mike James, Balsall Common, Solihull, West Midlands.

Ian Taylor celebrates scoring against Leeds United at Wembley in 1996.

One of the fun things I remember about Ian Taylor was his celebrations with Tommy Johnson when either of them scored a goal. My Aston Villa supporting friends and I used to copy striking a statuesque pose in the playground after scoring a goal at lunch time. He always seemed to be having such a laugh with Tommy and the supporters fed off it.

We hadn't beaten Liverpool for years until early 1997 when Ian Taylor scored the winner in front of the Holte End with less than 10 minutes to go. I just remember the noise when it went in after Andy Townsend crossed the ball and it found its way to Ian about eight yards out and he just blasted it into the roof of the net. It was great to finally get one over on them and fitting that Ian Taylor should be the one to get the goal.

Another goal that sticks in my head was his acrobatic effort in a 2–0 win against Wimbledon at Villa Park in 1998. It was Paul Merson's debut for the club and he had opened the scoring after missing a penalty via the rebound. Earlier in that same match Alan Thompson had also missed a penalty. Ian sealed the victory with a great winner during the brilliant 12 match unbeaten League start under John Gregory.

One of the memorable Aston Villa wins during that 12 match unbeaten Premier League start was the 2–0 away victory over Coventry City the following month. Much like the goal he scored against Liverpool the previous season Ian blasted the ball home from seven yards out. His second was a tap in after clever Merson play in what was personally one of my most memorable seasons.

Ian Taylor will first and foremost always be remembered for his brilliant volley in the League Cup Final against Leeds United at Wembley. It was my first visit to Wembley having missed the previous Cup Final in 1994 and I was smack bang in line with the penalty box on the side of the area he struck it from so I witnessed just how good the technique was. I remember it like it was yesterday and Ian contributed to what is one of the best days of my life.

Ian was always described as the workhorse of the team during his time at the club, a magnificent servant and one of us – a Villa fan.

Mark Jones, Birmingham (Aston Villa employee).

Bryan Small started out as a trainee at his hometown club Aston Villa and made 35 appearances for the first team. At international level he was capped 12 times for the England Under-21 team.

My abiding memory of playing for Villa is obviously my debut in the 1991–92 season against Everton at Goodison. We won the game 2–0, and it was the most important match I have ever played in really. I remember the build up to the match and once I knew I was picked for the team that was it really. I was thrilled to bits that I was making my debut for my hometown club and obviously we got the result as well.

I was also picked for the England Under-21 team and made 12 appearances for them and they were good times as well. When I first got mentioned for the Under-21s I was chuffed to bits. Although I can't remember who we played on my international debut, it was still very important for me. I can't even remember where we played it was that long ago. Unfortunately, I didn't make the step up into the senior squad but I was very proud to play for the Under-21s.

Bryan Small, former Villa defender, 1990–96.

I have supported the Villa since 1961 so have seen a lot of players. When I was at junior school in the early 1960s my best friend at school was Stuart Baxter the son of Bill Baxter, the Villa coach (1957–67) and they lived in a Villa owned house in Wylie Road, Witton. Bill Baxter would come and watch the school team play (Hawthorne School) and give us a bit of football coaching. It must have been good because we won the League that year. Incidentally, Stuart Baxter had an interesting career in football management abroad.

My other story is that the Villa trained at the HP Sauce ground in Grange Road, Erdington and we would often go to watch them train. That was in the days of Colin Withers, Tony Hateley and Mick Wright, It's ironic because I went later in life to work for HP Sauce and played many a game on my heroes pitch. Also the Spain squad used it as their training ground for the 1966 World Cup.

Stephen Owens, Castle Vale, Birmingham.

My love of Aston Villa has gone hand in hand with my passion for collecting Villa badges. I bought my first badge back in 1967 and have been collecting ever since. Around 15 years ago I joined the Association of Football Badge Collectors (AFBC) and regularly attend badge fairs across the country, picking up a number of gems and making friends with many a passionate collector. I have built up an extensive collection of Aston Villa badges and tend to focus on enamel badges. At last count I had around 2,000 Villa badges and continue to add to my collection on an almost daily basis.

My first great game at Villa Park was the FA Cup replay on 29 January 1969 against Southampton of the First Division. Until then the only big crowds I had seen at Villa Park were against Small Heath (Birmingham City). It was a night game, the crowd was 59,084 and the score was 2–1. The atmosphere was electric and I knew then that Aston Villa and Villa Park were special. However, it went downhill from there as we were relegated to the Third Division, but for me the Villa started to grow into a great side.

The first game of the season was Chesterfield away it was a great day out as we won 3–2 and my memory was that the Villa fans had packed the Chesterfield end. The terrace was made up of cinders or something similar and every time the Villa scored the crowd went crazy and a cloud of black dust went up and everyone ended up choking and looking like Al Jolson. Two seasons in the Third Division, a League Cup semi-final against Manchester United and 62,500 packed into Villa Park for the home leg and one of the greatest games I have ever seen followed by a trip to Wembley.

I personally loved our time in the Third Division and bought my first champions badge from the club shop. Ron Saunders arrived at the start of the 1974–75 season and we were promoted to the First Division. Who could forget the game at Hillsborough against Sheffield Wednesday when we won promotion with a 4–0 win. Ironically that game relegated Wednesday to the Third Division. Another great game never to be forgotten was when we won the League Cup beating Norwich City in the Final. What a season that was!

During my school years in the sixties I can never ever remember the Villa on Match of The Day and apart from Gerry Hitchens our team players were not exactly household names. By the time the 1980–81 season started we had a team of stars that everybody had heard of and we were on Match of The Day regularly.

It was a dream come true when we won the League. I saw the first game at Leeds United we won 2–1 and Peter Withe was a revelation. It was 'nip and tuck' with Ipswich Town all through the season and it went down to the wire at the last game of the season. We turned up in our hordes at Highbury to hope see the Villa beat Arsenal while Ipswich Town were also away at Middlesbrough who we had beaten at Villa Park the week before 3–0. We lost to Arsenal 2–0 and to be honest we were very poor on the day and never looked like winning. Everyone was down in the mouth, but then news of Ipswich Town losing at Middlesbrough changed the whole atmosphere. We had won the League at full time because Middlesbrough did us a great favour and beat Ipswich. A great day, a great season! The next season we were in the European Cup and it was another dream come true. In the first round we were up against FC Valur, the champions of Iceland and we won comfortably by 5–0 in the away leg and 2–0 at Villa Park. A few mates and I were already set for the final.

We gave the other away games a miss and made a big thing of the Final to be played in Rotterdam, Holland. In round two we beat Dynamo Berlin; round three Dynamo Kiev; semi-final Anderlecht. We had done it – the European Cup Final and a great team to play in Bayern Munich. There had been crowd trouble in Anderlecht so the club asked fans to travel by train from New Street Station to Rotterdam via the ferry and there was also a ban on alcohol.

A close friend of mine and fellow Villa fan Pete Williams made a telephone call to a mutual friend of ours called Mick Measey who was Gary Shaw's cousin and we managed to get two tickets. So off we went to Amsterdam on the Monday morning. We were crossing the North Sea with a ship full of Aston Villa fans all headed for Amsterdam drinking and dancing on the tables and the steward said to me that this was the quietest ship since Saturday that he had been on with Villa fans. When we arrived in Amsterdam it was like being in Birmingham – everywhere you went you bumped into Villa fans.

We had a great time in Amsterdam and travelled to Rotterdam on the morning of the match. A great party was going on in the city centre outside all the bars as the weather was excellent. We went to the match about 6pm as the ground was in the middle of nowhere. We played very well and kept Bayern Munich at bay then Peter With scored for the Villa and the rest is history. Champions of Europe and another dream come true. We watched them present the Cup to Dennis Mortimer and the lap of honour then off we went back to Rotterdam city centre for more celebrations. We ended up in a nightclub owned by a very amiable Jewish fellow and we drank the place dry. He came on the stage to say all he had left was Guinness but he halved the price and so the merriment went on until the early hours of the morning. This had been the greatest match I had ever seen. The only thing I had not seen the Villa win was the FA Cup but there is plenty of time. We finally managed to get to the Final in 2000 against Chelsea but it was not to be.

During all this time I have collected hard enamel Aston Villa badges, club badges, trophy badges, European competition badges, Stewards badges, Shareholders badges etc. I have also collected all the badges of the teams that play or have played in the Football League and also their supporters' club badges. I have a website where you can look at all my badges, over 27,000 people have looked at them to date.

Dave Jones, Earlswood, Solihull, West Midlands.
www.astonvillabadges.co.uk

Graham Denton lives in East Yorkshire with his wife and two children. He is a widely published children's poet, whose work has featured in over 30 UK publications. As an anthologist, his collections include *Silly Superstitions* (Macmillan Children's Books), *Giving You the 'Willies' (Delightfully Devilish Verse and Much, Much Worse!)* (Hands Up Books), *Wild! Rhymes that Roar* (Macmillan Children's Books), *Orange Silver Sausage* (Walker Books), *My Cat is in Love with the Goldfish* (A&C Black), and *When Granny Won Olympic Gold* (A&C Black) forthcoming in 2011. Two of his collections have received short-listings for the CLPE poetry award.

Why do I support Aston Villa? It's a question that I'm often asked even to this day, some 37 years since I first became a fully-fledged Villain, and claret-and-blue blood began coursing through my veins. Being born and raised in the suburbs of Hull, a club from the heart of the Midlands certainly was not a natural or obvious choice. Do we choose our clubs or do they choose us? In all honesty, I'm still not sure. I can't give one definite answer why Aston Villa.

As an eight, nine, and 10-year-old I did frequent Boothferry Park (Hull City's ground in those days), and Hull were a decent outfit at the time. However, I distantly recall seeing Villa topple the 'Tigers' 2–1 in April 1973, the first side I ever saw consign City to a home defeat. Perhaps it was that or perhaps it was coming from a suburban household, the lure of Hull City was never strong enough for me; I did not really feel like a 'Hull' person; my affinity to the club was never quite strong enough; I wanted to attach myself elsewhere and also be different from most of my peers, the majority of whom sported the colours of the white of Leeds or the red of Liverpool.

Whatever it was, from 1974 onwards (which just happened to be Villa's centenary year) Villa were my team and, as the saying on one of my Villa enamel badges goes, 'I'm Villa till I die'. In the last 37 years I have, of course, witnessed many highs and lows, but that's part of the deal of being a football supporter; you learn to accept it. It was not always so easy; as a young boy I suffered terribly when Villa lost (sometimes to the point of tears); I sulked for days on end. Conversely, though, when they won I was happy as the proverbial Larry. Talking of Larry, I must mention Larry Canning. One of the joys of being, in the main, an armchair supporter (I only got to go to Villa Park a couple of times a season back then), was listening to Larry Canning on the radio. Larry Canning, in a role now filled by Pat Murphy, was the Midlands reporter. Canning was an ex-Villa player, having joined the club in September 1948 and made 39 League appearances, scoring three goals from right-half. And he was obviously a Villa fan and though he did his best to disguise his affinities it was obvious that he suffered the defeats like the rest of the Villa fans and celebrated when Villa were victorious.

It's hard to believe now in these times of 24/7 football exposure, but football programmes on both TV and the radio were at a premium in the 1970s and 1980s, mercifully so, in my opinion. The long-running 'Sport on 2' was virtually all we had, by way of radio coverage, and my little transistor was the most prized possession of my childhood. I loved to hear Canning's voice. In fact, I loved to hear any mention of Villa in those days. Even to the point where I would set up my tape recorder next to the radio and record Larry giving out the Villa team news on a Saturday afternoon! Teams were 'teams' back then (not the 20 or 30 man squads you have now), so injuries and suspensions were rare, as were wholesale team changes, let alone 'squad rotation'.

I was always fascinated to discover if the Villa XI were the same as the previous week, and if not who'd replaced whom. Often it was a total newcomer you'd never heard of, a reserve, or some young Scot they'd signed in the summer without you knowing. Even the selection of the one sub was a source of much anticipation. Everything to do with the pre-match build-up was exciting to my young mind.

This was also a time that came long before the days of the monopoly of the so-called 'Top Four' that dominates football in this more predictable era. Even though Liverpool and, for a season or two, Nottingham Forest were top dogs and inevitable favourites to win the League title, the hopes of 'other teams' of toppling them were still high. Villa was among those 'other teams'. Under Ron Saunders they were a consistent outfit and finished fourth, eighth, eighth again and seventh from 1976–77 onwards. I sensed that Saunders was building a team that could challenge the best, even though it broke my heart to see the likes of John Gidman, John Deehan, Andy Gray and Ray Graydon all disappear elsewhere. And so it proved in 1980–81. Villa became champions of the old First Division for the first time since 1909–10. For those of us old enough to remember, it was an undoubted high point for all supporters. I do feel, like many others, that Villa's remarkable achievement in that season has been somewhat unfairly overlooked. The fact that they won the First Division with a squad of just 14 players (of whom seven were ever present) was an astonishing feat in itself, and one which is highly unlikely to be repeated ever again in the modern game. Maybe it was the fact that runners-up Ipswich were everyone's favourite second team; they supposedly played the more attractive football with their three-pronged strike force of Gates, Brazil and Mariner, and the mercurial skills of the Dutch duo Mühren and Thijssen pulling the strings in midfield.

The fact remains that had the three-points-for-a-win rule been in place (as it was for the first time the following season), Villa would have won the title by an even greater margin than they actually did do. In short, they won more matches – 26 – than anyone else and were worthy champions.

Going on to triumph in the European Cup the following season only proved what a solid 'team' they were. True, there were no real individuals in the side but each player was a vital cog in a very smooth and highly efficient machine that on its day was capable of producing some scintillating soccer. They certainly didn't lack flair. Players like Gordon Cowans, Tony Morley and Gary Shaw were often breathtaking to watch. Winning the European Cup in 1982 was yet another exceptional feat, given the loss of Ron Saunders in the February of that triumphant year. Again, maybe that achievement has been lessened somewhat (by others, certainly not Villa fans) by the fairly rapid decline in Villa's fortunes in the years that followed (they were relegated to the then Second Division only five years after being champions of Europe). Who knows? But the history books don't lie; Aston Villa were First Division champions in the 1980–81 season, and deservedly so. Although there were many, one highlight of that title-winning season in particular stands out for me.

On 25 April 1981 I stood on the Holte End terrace at Villa Park as Villa took on Middlesbrough on a drizzly day in the Midlands. Villa won the game 3–0, which kept them ahead of their nearest title rivals Ipswich Town with one game to go. Halfway through the game a buzz went around the ground that Ipswich had gone behind to Manchester City, meaning that the title was now in Villa's grasp; however, it was not to be. Ipswich had actually won 1–0 that day. A draw in Villa's final game of the season at Highbury would guarantee victory in the title race. Records will show that Villa were beaten 2–0 at the Arsenal that day (a game I sat at home in East Yorkshire listening to, with my radio glued to my ear as tightly as I dare); it was slightly anti-climatic but with little consequence; their closest rivals from Portman Road had also lost, meaning Villa could not be caught on points despite Ipswich having games in hand. Ipswich's defeat came at the hands of the very same Middlesbrough team I had seen thrashed at Villa Park in the previous week. Both the 'Boro goals against Ipswich in a 2–1 victory came late on and were scored by Bosko Jancovic.

Some years later I heard a rumour that Jancovic had returned to his native Yugoslavia and died during fighting in the Balkans War. Other reports claimed that he left football to begin a law practice back in Sarajevo, Bosnia and that he had he died in 1993 of a cancer-related illness just a couple years after the Balkan Wars started. Whatever the truth, I can't help but feel a small debt of gratitude to the man who, while by no means single-handedly, certainly helped steer the Villa ship towards that golden shore in 1981. That glorious Saturday in May was undoubtedly one of the highlights, if not *the* highlight, of my time as a fan of the 'greatest team in the world'. Hopefully, there'll be many, many more yet to come.

Graham Denton, Hull, East Yorkshire.
www.handsup.karoo.net

I haven't got any notable 'stories' to tell as such; however, I have a few significant memories I have encountered over the years whilst watching the Villa home and away:

- ⚽ I will never forget the first time I walked up the infamous Holte End steps when I was about 10 years old and thinking how long it seemed to reach the top!
- ⚽ Who could ever forget the game (against Arsenal) when Santa got stuck on the roof?
- ⚽ The never-ending change of intro music to when the teams walked out – from the terrible 'Thunderbirds' theme to inspiring videos on the big screen!

- The days when the crazy Alpay used to play centre back, and whenever someone scored at the North Stand end he would give them a piggy-back ride back to Villa's half (mostly Paul Merson).
- Juan Pablo Angel's first goal against Coventry City – which subsequently sent them down! He was probably my favourite Villa player ever, despite his ups and downs, he brightened up Villa Park every time he played. Never forget that goal he scored against Chelsea in the cup.
- The numerous funny songs the Holte End crowd has produced: 'Sit down potato head', 'Sit down Pinocchio', 'Paul McGrath my lord...' and some others I can't repeat obviously.
- I used to go to Bodymoor Heath training ground when I was younger, and couldn't believe my eyes when I saw David Ginola and Mustapha Hadji both having a 'fag' outside!
- Going to Leicester's old ground, Filbert Street, and watching George Boateng and Paul Dickov have a scrap at the final whistle – resulting in Boateng launching Dickov's boot over the stadium roof as it was so small.
- Taking my girlfriend to her first ever football match and reassuring her that she has missed out all her life, to which Villa lost 3–0 at home to Middlesbrough in the pouring rain and was the worst match I have ever been to. She has never been since.

Patrick Barber, Coleshill, North Warwickshire.

Supporting Aston Villa in the late 1960s was a painful experience for a 14-year-old schoolboy. Years of neglect and lack of ambition from a once-famous club had taken its toll, a crumbling ground and even crumblier team had been take over by Doug Ellis, whose appointment of the ebullient Tommy Docherty had initially had the short-term effect of lifting everyone, and results improved so dramatically that relegation was staved off and there was a huge wave of unfounded optimism for the new season. However, that season proved to be the worst in Aston Villa's history as the unthinkable happened...Villa were relegated to the Third Division!

But those two seasons in the third tier of English football awakened a sleeping giant; a Wembley appearance and a record-breaking points total was achieved as Villa swept to the Championship and our supporters, starved of success for so many years, swarmed back to Villa Park in their thousands.

For many supporters of a certain age, those Third Division days hold a special place in our hearts, as Villa feasted on goals and victories. It was such an exciting time to be a Villa fan, and although ten years later the club achieved the ultimate in European club football on a warm night in Rotterdam, somehow nothing ever quite matched the excitement of massive victories at places like Oldham, Chesterfield and Notts County, and the hero worshiping of Andy Lochhead and Bruce Rioch.

That first, shocking season of Third Division football (1970–71) began with a win at Chesterfield, where there were so many Villa fans in the away end (which usually became most of the stadiums in most away grounds) at Saltergate, that manager Vic Crowe was asked to talk to the fans by megaphone to stop the crowd surges, and also ended at Villa Park against the same Derbyshire club famous for the crooked Church spire. In between were shocks…humiliating defeats at places like Walsall, Plymouth, Bournemouth, Tranmere, Torquay, Rochdale and Bury (in fact we couldn't beat Walsall in four attempts!)…Huge crowds including 55,000 against Pelé's Santos of Brazil in a friendly match under lights powered by generators because of the power strike at the time…Wembley Cup Final defeat to the mighty Spurs when Villa's fans drowned out their illustrious opponents…and massive wins like 6–0 at Oldham and goals galore from Lochhead, Willie Anderson, Ray Graydon, Bruce Rioch, Chico Hamilton and even Charlie Aitken!

On Saturday 29 April 1972, Aston Villa were confirmed as Third Division champions, Andy Lochhead was presented with the Midlands 'Footballer of the Year' trophy, and Villa's FA Youth Cup Winners (including future stars Brian Little and John Gidman) paraded the trophy around the pitch before Torquay were stuffed 5–1 by the senior team. In front of ITV's *Star Soccer* cameras, Villa only needed a point to make sure of the Championship, but they took the Devon club apart and the star of the show was 17-year-old Youth player called Brian Little.

After an early goal from Geoff Vowden, the party atmosphere started at first, Little set up Andy Lochhead for a tap-in and his 25th goal of the season, then, after an own goal, the youngster made it 4–0 himself with a close range shot. Former Villa player Dick Edwards scored a consolation goal, but Vowden scored another to make it 5–1 as Villa left the field to 38,000 fans chanting, 'Champions, Champions'.

In that last game the following Friday, Villa were presented with the Third Division trophy on the pitch as they beat Chesterfield 1–0 with new signing Ian Ross getting the goal in front of nearly 46,000 fans.

So ended a season to remember – champions, FA Youth Cup-winners, record points in a season, record wins in a season, record Third Division attendances, and a manager of the year award for Vic Crowe.

For a 14-year-old kid from Billesley in Birmingham, it was a truly special time to be a Villa fan.

Mike Davies, Solihull, West Midlands.

I was five years old when my older brother came home from school one day and for no apparent reason said that he supported Aston Villa, so I thought, 'yeah, so will I'. Thank God he didn't say he supported 'the other lot' (Blues).

I've been supporting Aston Villa for 51 years now and started attending Villa Park at the age of eight. In May 1963, in fact a 2–0 defeat against

Nottingham Forest was the first match that I attended with my dad towards the end of the 1962–63 season and even though we lost the game the bug had bit me and I absolutely loved it.

I had to wait another six months before my dad took me to watch another game, but what a game that was – the 4–0 drubbing of Manchester United (November 1963). I remember travelling on the Outer Circle number 11 bus to get to Witton Square where we got off and made our way to the ground. I can't remember exactly what part of the ground we watched the match from but it was certainly a memorable game. A headed goal from Tony Hateley within the first minute or two set the scene and three more Villa goals, the Denis Law sending off for kicking Alan Deakin in the face while he was on the ground but the one moment that stood out for me was when Charlie Aitken (the man's a 'legend') went deep inside his own half pushed the ball past Bobby Charlton's right hand side, ran past his United opponent's left hand side and managed to beat him to the ball – pure magic.

During the 1960s I used to go down with my dad and we normally stood on the Holte End, with the odd excursion into the Lower Trinity Stand. We wouldn't attend every game but would probably go to at least half of the home matches in a season. My first away match was also with my dad and it was the game against the Blues in Feb 1965, an encounter which we won 1–0 with a goal from Barry Stobart.

Saturday 16 August 1969, for me it was a landmark date in history – my first Villa away game without my dad being with me. A friend at that time and myself got on the Villa football special from New Street station to Huddersfield. It was a 3–4 carriage diesel multiple unit (DMU) that wasn't exactly first class travel (anyone who used to go on these would know what I'm on about), but nevertheless it was straight from Birmingham into Huddersfield, no changing of trains and it was cheap. This was the season of 'The Doc', claret shirts with light blue cuffs and collars and light blue shorts; a change strip of yellow and blue and the home programme's cover alternating between claret and light blue; this was the season of so much anticipation. It was not a great game if I was honest and to make matters worse we lost it 2–0 but my most vivid recollection of the day was when our goalkeeper (Evan Williams) just after the half-time interval asked the supporters in the Cowshed End behind his goal if anyone knew how Wolves were getting on. I was a bit surprised but as he was on loan from Wolves at the time I thought I'd let him off.

I went to four more away matches during that season; Cardiff – we lost 4–0; Oxford 2–2; Blues – we won 2–0 and it was great to be at our only away win of the season and to witness one of Bruce Rioch's magical left footed wonder strikes and Leicester. I remember the Leicester match quite well. It was a rather wet late Saturday afternoon when my dad and I made our way to New Street station for the evening kick off. British Rail had to put on 2–3 special trains that evening because when the only one designated 'special' left there were still masses of Villa fans left on the platform. Of course this was the match of the infamous 'goal that never was'. Pat McMahon hit a ferocious 20–25yd drive that flew in-between the outstretched left hand of Peter Shilton and his left sided post and then in a blink of an eye it came back past Shilton and back into the field of play. The referee who was a grey haired older man (who would have surely been past retiring age in this modern era of football) was somewhere near the half way line and had no chance of determining if the ball had crossed the line or not so play was waved on much to the concern of the Villa players and supporters in the crowd. Who knows, if the goal had been given we may have gone on to have won the match and that in turn could have affected our League position at the end of the season. We went on to win our last two matches (both of them at home) and we were only two points behind Charlton (who stayed up) but we had the better goal average (it is called goal difference nowadays) yet we were the ones who fell through the trap door to the Third Division for the first time in our history.

I would think most Villa fans of that era, if they were honest with themselves, enjoyed those two seasons in the Third Division, not because of the standard of football that we were playing – although it was true to say we started winning more than we lost which was something new to us younger supporters, but because of the away days where we seemed to double (sometimes even treble) the home team's average attendance gate and generally had a good time at those grounds. Again I didn't go to all but some did stand out more so than others like the two away games played at Swansea; the 4–4 draw at Port Vale in our second season in the Third Division, but I guess two more than most stood out for me and they were both from that second season in that division and they were the trips to Notts County and Mansfield. Notts County was memorable because they were a well fancied side and along with us and Bournemouth were one of the favourites to gain promotion. I would say that there were at least about 15,000–20,000 Villa fans that made the trip to the East Midlands that day which swelled the attendance to 34,208. Most of us were crowded into the large stand that ran the length of the pitch opposite their main stand. We cheered the lads onto a memorable 3–0 victory which really helped our promotion push. Mansfield was memorable because that was the night promotion was secured, although we only drew the match 1–1 (Geoff Vowden was our goalscorer) it was enough to gain automatic promotion.

Three seasons later we were celebrating a return to the First Division under Ron Saunders and playing some very attractive football during the course of that season, as well as winning the League Cup. My away trip to Blackpool during that promotion winning season was quite an eventful one as I recollect. It started off with the coach journey from just outside the old Mulberry Bush pub by the Bull Ring with the coaches due to leave at about

9.30am. There were three coaches lined up so me and my mate, John 'Ducky' Doyle went and sat on coach number 3. With about 10–15 minutes before departure time it was obvious our coach would not fill up so those of us who were on it were asked to get onto coach number 2. Now these were the days of just turning up and paying your money and that was that. So the two coaches got under way and I believe in all the confusion of transferring coaches my mate and I must have forgot to pay our fare (or the organiser forgot to ask us – it was one or the other). When we arrived at Blackpool we were told by one of the organisers that the coach would depart at midnight. This immediately got the driver's back up as he obviously knew nothing about this and said he would be departing earlier than that and it would be no later than 10pm. Eventually after some negotiation we were told the coach would leave Blackpool at 11pm so a happy medium had been struck, or so we thought. Before the match a number of us sampled the delights of the fun fair and of course indulged in a few pre-match beers. The game wasn't bad either as we won 3–0 thus keeping us bang on course for promotion. In fact in the large open bank of terracing behind the one goal where the majority of Villa fans were news started spreading that we had gained promotion because Sunderland had lost. This proved to be untrue, but we didn't have to wait too long before promotion became reality as it was gained the following Wednesday (appropriately) night at Hillsborough via a 4–0 win.

But back to Blackpool, after the match 'Duck' and myself found a pub to celebrate the victory in and then moving on from there found a working men's club that allowed us in to watch Villa on Match of the Day (I think we were the second game on that night). We knew this would be cutting it fine to get back to the coach for 11 pm but we took the risk anyway. As it was we just made it back to the coach park for 11 pm only to find our coach had already departed. We were not the only Villa supporters stuck in the proverbial rut but luckily there were two other coaches still left on the coach park that would be heading back down to Birmingham. I don't know how we managed to do it but we 'blagged' our way onto one of them and got home into Birmingham city centre in time to take one of the all night bus services back to my mate's flat. So all the way to Blackpool and back for 10p – the tip I gave the driver of the coach coming back ... it was all I had left.

The first season we were back in the First Division I had started to play in goal for a Saturday afternoon amateur football team, so Villa matches went on the back burner, until the day of the big derby game against Blues at Villa Park, the first time the two teams had met in the top flight for nearly 10 and a half years. I was due to meet up with the rest of the team at the White Hart in Tile Cross at lunch time (we had a Cup replay) the only trouble was no one else turned up. A number of the lads who would have turned up at the pub had decided to go down to watch the big game. On realising the fact that I wouldn't be playing football that afternoon I started asking around some friends if they had a spare ticket for the match. By some miracle I managed to obtain a ticket so on leaving my kit bag at a friend's house I made my way with some friends down to Villa Park and I was immensely pleased that I did as goals from Chico Hamilton and Brian Little gave Villa a 2–1 victory in front of almost 54,000 people.

Incidentally, after that episode with the Saturday football team I didn't play for them again, in fact the team disintegrated and played no more matches that season. So my Saturday afternoons were freed up and I could go down to Villa Park once more and indeed went one better by going to quite a few of the away matches again too. There would be a group of 10–12 of us that clubbed together and hired a mini transit from Bristol Street Motors in town. One of us would pick it up on a Friday evening or early Saturday morning and drive it to a meeting point on the Saturday morning. I went to 11 of the away matches that season, starting with the Middlesbrough game (where Andy Gray made his debut) and the last one I went to was Tottenham away. It was another one of those seasons when Villa didn't win one away game so it was pretty disheartening from the footballing point of view but we did have some fun on our travels. We generally arrived at a pub reasonably close to the away ground and indulged in the pre-match drink before it filled up with too many of the home supporters and some of the group took to putting on monkey masks and then hanging their heads out of the windows of the transit coach generally to the amazement of the locals.

Happy days!

Jim Weaver, Bournville, Birmingham.

I became a Villa fan through my father, when he came over to England from India in the 1950s. My father went to the 1957 FA Cup Final. My elder brother went to the 1971 League Cup Final, but my father wouldn't let me go as he said I was too young and I cried my eyes out. However, he got me my first season ticket when I was a bit older in the 1975–76 season when I was eight years old. We were in the Witton Lane Stand, Door M, Row A, Seats 162 and 163 and we had those seats for a long, long time after that.

I remember we turned up at Villa Park for the end of season awards night and saw Eric

The 1957 FA Cup Final programme.

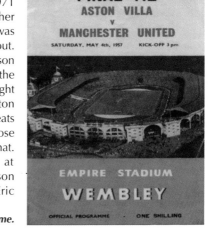

Morecombe and Ernie Wise presenting Ron Saunders with the Manager of the Year Award for 1974–75. My first match as a season ticket holder was against that great Leeds United side managed by Don Revie, who were Champions only a season before (1973–74) and they beat us 2–1 in our first season back in the First Division.

My biggest memory my dad gave me though, was when we went to Blackpool in the season we gained promotion (1974–75 season) and Brian Little scored to make it 3–0. Tom Seiger was a business partner of my dad's and a good friend and he became the Chairman of Blackpool back then and he took us round Bloomfield Road and invited us to watch the game with him. We could have got promoted that day but it did not work out as Sunderland and Norwich were still in the hunt. It was my first away trip with my dad at the age of eight. Fantastic!!

Years later, when we went to Leicester City in the season we were going for the Championship in 1981, we sat in the director's box as my dad had contacts in the textile industry. We had a meal in the director's box and saw the lads come from behind to beat Leicester 4–2, with Peter Withe scoring two, Bremner and Morley getting the other two. I think Ipswich lost at home that day. I remember it well, as it was a strange day because I saw in the window in the block of flats opposite the ground that Aldaneti had won the Grand National. Of course, only a few weeks later, we travelled upto Highbury along with 25,000 other Villa fans to see our worse performance of the season but Bosco Jankovic won it for us in the end as Middlesbrough beat Ipswich. We were all supporting Middlesbrough that day.

Charlie Singh, Sutton Coldfield, West Midlands.

I went along to Villa Park on Saturday 26 July 1969. This was supposed to be the beginning of a bright new dawn for Aston Villa. We had been relegated to the old Second Division a couple of seasons previously, but had appointed Tommy Docherty as our new manager, so hopes were high for a quick return to the top flight.

It was a bright sunny day and as part of our preparation for the new season we had arranged a friendly with the Italian Under-23 side. As my mates and I stood on the Trinity Road terraces the music on the loud speakers died away and the Italians took to the pitch in their yellow and blue strip, all tanned and fit, we gave them a volley of 'boos' just to let them know how we felt. We carried on booing as Villa had yet to take the pitch, then an odd thing happened. As we looked round the pitch there was a striking resemblance between these Italians and certain Villa players, Then out ran the other team all in blue. Yes the Italian Under-23 team. This was the first time Villa had ever worn a yellow strip and some of us hoped it would be the last, and the tans were due to Villa just returning from Atlanta in the USA!

As a footnote that bright new dawn turned into a nightmare once the season started for real and Docherty was eventually sacked and this great club was relegated to the Third Division for the first time in the clubs proud history.

Michael d'Abreu, Birmingham.

The year was 2007 and I was studying at University College London. In fact, and to be precise, I was in the middle of my examination period and I was about to sit a very important exam and obviously I was very nervous. All of a sudden my phone rang with a very short and strange number which I didn't recognise. I didn't know whether to answer it or not, as I was about to walk into my examination, but I thought I may as well before turning off the phone.

The guy on the other end of the line asked me 'Is this Matt Walker?' to which I replied 'Yes, who is this please?' He went on to ask me if I remembered entering a competition online with '32-Red', who were the shirt sponsors of Aston Villa at that time. I had to think hard about it, but I replied that I did remember answering a few questions online, on the official Aston Villa website, but that was about all I could remember. The man responded by laughing before telling me that I was actually the winner of the competition, which now meant that myself and a guest would be playing football on Villa Park, with some former Villa stars, as part of the 25 years of winning the European Cup celebrations! I couldn't believe my ears, as he went on to inform me that my guest and I would be welcomed at the gate, before being taken to the dressing room to get ready for the game of our lives!

As you can imagine, I wanted to know more and asked loads of questions until I realised that I was now late for my exam and so I made my excuses and thanked the man from '32-Red' for his call.

So off I raced to the exam hall. I was very late and the exam had started, but I sat down in order to sit the exam with a huge smile on my face. To be honest, I just couldn't concentrate at all, as all I kept thinking about was my dream coming true of playing football on Villa Park; however, when my exam results came, I just about scraped it!

Matt Walker, London.

Gerry Hitchens was my dad's best mate when he lived opposite us in Halesowen. How he came to have it I will never know, but in those rather different times, somehow Gerry ended up borrowing the League Cup sometime before the Final (even though he did not play in the Final). During the time that he had it, the complete Hitchens family were going to be away and, therefore, their house was not going to be occupied. Not wishing to risk being responsible for having the Cup stolen, Gerry asked my parents to look after it, and for one glorious weekend the Cup stayed at our house.

Paul Farrington, Halesowen, West Midlands.

When I was eight my uncle took me with his team Wishaw Athletic on the mini bus to see the League Cup Final v Everton in 1977. It was the worst game ever!! My abiding memory was walking up Wembley Way before the game and a group of Villa fans holding a ticket tout literally by the ankles, hanging him over the side (a big drop) and shaking all of the money out of his pockets!

Mark Burke, former Aston Villa midfielder (1987).

Back in the 1950s my father used to manage a repair garage in Hockley. There were several Villa players who used the garage. Pat Saward among them. Because of this we always had two tickets for the half way line row ZZ in the Trinity Road Stand. I was not very happy as a past master at moaning even when I was very young, he gave in and took me too. Lifting me over the turnstile and slipping the attendant some coins. There were always spare seats in that area back in those days.

Later in life I use to stand in the Witton End so I could feel the wall of sound come down the pitch from the Holte End. During a League Cup semi-final involving Manchester United, I was standing in the same stand as the opposition, not wearing a scarf on that night! Then Andy Lochhead rose above the defence and scored. I leapt in the air with my arms raised. My flat hat disappeared and lots of fans were looking at me as I tried to make myself small. Then a fan with hate written all over his face was climbing over people to get to me. I froze. Then out of the blue came a police officer who saw what was about to happen and grabbed him just before he got to me. I then moved to another part of the stand. When the second goal went in, outwardly, I was motionless, just a faint smile.

For the 1977 Final I was given two tickets from a contact at Stoke City Football Club having promised to sell them at more than face value (I only needed one). Travelling down to Wembley, I stopped at a motorway service station for a comfort break and I overheard two Villa fans talking about how much an extra ticket would cost as they only had one between them. 'How much?'

'Face value', I said! Good deed done. If only the Final had been worth watching!!

Brian Thompson, Rodès, South of France.

I have been a supporter since 1946 and was there when we played Derby County before a record crowd of 76,588. The most memorable thing about the 1957 FA Cup Final was Peter McParland shoulder charging Ray Wood, who was injured and then had to play on the left wing for Manchester United.

The building we used in Victoria Road was owned by the Solicitors, Lovesey, Bourne and Haywood. Mr Lovesey was a Director at the Villa at the time and was the man who apparently arranged the transfer of Gerry

Hitchens to Inter Milan. I still consider Gerry to be the best centre-forward to play for Villa.
Ron Hibbs, Birmingham.

I played against Bobby Thomson when he was playing for RAF Bridgnorth and I was playing right-half for RAF Cosford. This took place at Molineux, perhaps at the peak of my football career. I have a loser's medal and I seem to remember Thomson scored a hat-trick against us. All this was during my National Service in the RAF. The other interesting thing here is that the other Thompson (Peter) with a 'P' went on the play for Wrexham and Derby County. Now a few notes on my muted trumpet. During my football days I played with and against three future international footballers. These were Ron Flowers, who was also stationed at Cosford, Ray Parry who was in my RAF group and I also played against Mel Charles who was stationed at the Army Camp at Donnington in Shropshire. This was one of the few times that I have been able to relate this information as most people have never heard of the players with the exception of Ron Flowers who was in the Alf Ramsey World Cup squad. So how near did I get? Well, I wasn't even on the subs bench as they did not exist....Well there it is...well not quite, as I also played as a kid (before National Service) for Boldmere St Michaels and had trials with Workington Town just before the immortal Bill Shankly became the manager there. On leaving the RAF I signed for the Blues, and that is where my career fizzled out, as I then went to university.
Morris Stephens, Aspiran, Herault, South of France.

My Great Grandfather, James Rowberry (known all his adult life as 'Jack') owned a beef butcher's shop at the bottom of Gravelly Hill. My parents' generation calculated it was on the site of the third supporting pillar along of what is now the Aston Expressway (known all its adult life as 'Spaghetti Junction'!) Until I came along, followed by my brother, Neil, no one in the family ever showed any interest in football. However, several of the Villa players used to call in at Rowberry's, in particular after they'd been paid on a Friday, for their Sunday joint. My grandfather seemed to have been well-known in the community (which it was, then) and my mother was known locally as 'The Butcher's Babby'. My Grandfather enjoyed the banter with those players who called in. (Neither Neil nor I can be certain of who did or who did not call in). We don't know of any single occasion, but evidently my grandfather – who enjoyed a bet and took these things seriously – derided Villa's chances of winning anything that season, and said he'd stake the team to their Sunday joints if they actually did win the Second Division Championship. I don't know that he stood to win anything if they failed, and he wasn't noted for benevolence or publicity stunts, so my guess is that he did not know what he was talking about. (It occurs to me that he may not even have known they'd been relegated). No doubt the players

J. Rowberry butchers in Gravelly Hill, Birmingham.

would have enjoyed this aspect, since he was not slow at voicing his opinions. As we know, Villa did win the Championship that year and the players held him to his word. However, as each called in, including, almost certainly, players that did not normally go home via Gravelly Hill, they were made to sign a sheet that was kept behind the counter, so that he wouldn't compound his error. Why my mum ended up with the sheet, I have no idea, except that she would, by then, be the only one of the five children still to be at school, and the sheet may have been torn from one of her books.

My grandfather died in 1954 and the shop was taken over by my Uncle Frank until a Compulsory Purchase Order (now, there's a phrase that rings of the sixties!) put an end to it. By way of postscript, in the season 1959–60, when Villa were again in the Second Division, Peter McParland was my hero. He, too, called in at the shop every week and my Uncle Frank got him to sign a drawing I'd done. He went further, and kindly filled two pages of my autograph book with signatures of the first team and reserves and of Joe Mercer for me. And we won it again, didn't we, after a tussle with Cardiff City.

Jack Miller, Liverpool.

As a life long Villa supporter, my claim to fame is that I must be one of the very few (if not the only one) to be at Villa Park when we had our record high attendance, and also our lowest attendance.

In 1945, the FA Cup made a welcome return. For the first and only time, the competition was organised on a two-leg basis. Both First and Second Division clubs competed in regionalised North and South Sections, with Villa playing in the latter. A record 76,588 Villa Park crowd watched the quarter-final home game against Derby County on 2 March 1946. Villa led 3–2 with only four minutes to play, thanks to goals from George Edwards, Bob Iverson and Frank Broome, but Peter Doherty equalised and Sammy Crooks snatched Derby's winner.

Along with many small boys, I remember being passed over the heads of the men on the open terrace at the Witton End (long before the North Stand was built). We were passed down to the very front to peer through the iron railings to watch the game at ground level.

More recently, after the triumph of winning the European Cup on 26 May 1982, the following season on 15 September we played our first-round European Cup match against Turkish club Besiktas. It was played behind closed doors at Villa Park as a punishment for crowd trouble in Brussels at the previous season's semi-final against Anderlecht. I was a Communications Engineer at the time, and was allowed into the ground as part of a small team supplying telephone and radio links for the press in this country, all over Europe and Turkey. Dozens of fans waited outside the gates in Trinity Road to hear news of the game, and several hundred caught a bit of the action by standing on the steep grass bank opposite, and looking through the gap between the old Trinity Road stand and the Holte End. Villa won the game 3–1 with goals from Peter Withe, Tony Morley and Dennis Mortimer.
Peter Stokes, Quinton, Birmingham.

I was born in Rowley Regis and was living there with my parents at the time of these stories (I am now 75 years old). My father was a cousin of Tommy Weston, left back in the 1913 and 1920 FA Cup finals. Tommy Smart, Weston's full back partner in the 1920 Final also lived locally. He was another great character. He often used to show me his winners' (1920) and losers' (1924) medals. He said when he was given his losers' medal in 1924 he told the rest of the team he didn't want a winners' medal as he already had one of those. He used to cycle from Blackheath to Villa Park (about eight or nine miles) to train every day. He also said he wouldn't dream of playing a match without two pints of beer and two penny worth of chips inside him. I have been following Villa since the war years. I could give you many memories of matches but instead I can contribute several off field stories.

When Villa last won the FA Cup in 1957 I was lucky to see every match including replays and the Final itself. I have several memories from after the games. Villa drew at Luton in the third round and after the game the team travelled back to Birmingham on the same train as the fans. They rarely went by coach then. The train was packed and my friend and I were

Peter Stokes was reporting on the European Cup game on 15 September 1982 against Turkish club Besiktas. Fans were banned from attending and the game was played behind closed doors.

standing in the corridor when an attractive lady came to use the toilet but immediately came back out saying the lock wouldn't work. Several minutes later she returned with Jimmy Dugdale and re-entered the toilet compartment, while Jim stood guard outside and told us what he would do to anyone who tried to enter while his wife was in there.

After the fourth round tie at Middlesbrough the team returned to Brum again on the same train as the supporters. Johnny Dixon had not been well but still played and scored the winner with a brilliant goal. We were waiting on the platform for the train when the team arrived at the station. Some fans immediately made for Johnny and hoisted him on to their shoulders and carried him around the platform until the train arrived. Then after the Final itself my friend and I decided to let the crowds make their way from the stadium and leave when the crush had finished. We decided to wait outside the players' entrance until the team came out to travel to their hotel for the celebrations. Wilfred Pickles, a famous radio personality of the time, passed us and said he was delighted that Villa had won. Then a small door opened in the dressing room and out came Con Martin. We had noticed that when the team were parading the trophy around the stadium that Stan Lynn had seen Con in the crowd and insisted that he join them on the pitch. Con had left Villa at end of the 1955–56 season after eight years great service to become player-manager of Waterford. We asked Con if he wished he had been playing and he stayed and chatted with us for a while and said he wished he could start his career all over again with Villa who were the greatest club in the world.

One last memory of Con Martin. I was in the Army doing my national service between 1954 and 1956. In 1955 I was stationed in Hampshire and I went to Portsmouth early in 1955 to see Villa in a First Division game. Martin was captain at the time and there was quite a dense fog during the game. Villa were losing 1–0 at half-time and on leaving the field Con could be heard begging the referee to abandon the game. In the second half Villa scored twice, the fog got worse and you could hardly see anything. The referee abandoned the game with only about 10 minutes left, whereupon Con told the ref that the fog was not that bad and the ref was out of order to abandon the game.

The game was replayed on an evening in April. I went to that game, bumped into Jimmy Easson the trainer in Portsmouth beforehand. We had a chat and he arranged for me to have a ticket. The game ended in a 2–2 draw.

Frank Allen, Droitwich, Worcestershire.

In August 1987 just after we were ignominiously relegated to the old Second Division and just after super Graham Taylor was appointed as our new manager I had the idea of taking my kittens to Villa Park. The idea was to hopefully bring us some much needed luck after having experienced such a disastrous time of it the previous season. (The things we do for the love of our team eh!) The black kitten (in the picture) was called 'Mombula Garry Thompson' after our great centre-forward of that era and the beautiful black and white kitten was called 'Rambo' after Alan McInally, our other great striker who we had just signed from Celtic. This 'special' visit

The black kitten called 'Mombula Garry Thompson' named after the centre-forward of that era. Here pictured on the Villa Park turf.

obviously did the trick for in an uncanny sort of way our claret and blue heroes then went from strength to strength that season, gaining promotion, and the rest is history, as they say.

Doug O'Brien, Erdington, Birmingham.

My family connections with Aston Villa go back quite a long way. My granddad fought in World War Two and came back with injuries which caused him long-term health problems, so life was tough for my grandmother and her two sons. The family lived in Witton Road, just around the corner from Villa Park in a house owned by Ansells Brewery, where my grandfather worked. To help make ends meet my nan took in washing, which included the Aston Villa team kit. My dad has told me stories of how he used to collect the players' kit from the dressing room and take it home for his mom to wash. It must have been really hard work, washing the mud and grass stains out of the heavy cotton by hand! This would probably have been during the late 1940s and early 1950s. My nan's house backed on to the Post Office Telephones Depot (which is now part of Villa Park) and my dad has also told me how he used to climb the fences into the depot and then into the Witton End to see the game for free!

The back of my nan's house was overlooked by Villa Park and at night, with the floodlights on, you could read a book in the garden! I vaguely remember the new 'AV' lights being installed – it would probably have been in the early seventies, with the huge lamps being hoisted into place and then tested when darkness fell.

When he got older, my dad went into business with his brother to form an electrical contracting business, S & A Pitt (Enterprises) Ltd. This would have been around the year I was born, 1960. They had a small shop in Witton Road, next to the billiard hall, where they sold electrical goods. Later they moved across the road into a larger unit where they also sold records, toys and other items. This shop has long been demolished and replaced with housing. By the late 1960s, as I recall, Aston Villa FC were going through something of a financial crisis and Chairman Doug Ellis appealed to supporters to rally round and help out. My dad and his brother did a lot of electrical work on the ground, including re-wiring much of the Trinity Road stand. In return they had advertisements put up around the ground, one of which was near the entrance to the Witton End. Because they sold records, my dad and his brother loaned discs to the club to play over the tannoy before and after matches, in return for which they got two free tickets. I sometimes used to accompany either my dad or uncle (who was not married and had no children of his own) to games. Carrying a box of records, we'd enter the Trinity Road stand through a door to the left of the main steps and make our way up to our seats in the upper tier. Collecting the box after the game, we'd quite often see players emerging from the dressing room and I was able to collect quite a few autographs from the likes of Willie Anderson, John Dunn, Charlie Aitken and many, many others. Sadly that book is long lost. I would have gone to quite a few matches in the late sixties but don't remember any now.

By the early seventies my dad and uncle had closed their shop and I had to pay to get into matches. This was when I became a 'Witton Ender' – probably around 1973. Although quite young, I attended matches on my own, which was easy as I had two sets of grandparents living in the area – my mom's parents lived in Deykin Avenue. I can still remember entering through terraces on Witton Lane and going up a short path to the terracing. On the left was a small kiosk on which was attached one of my dad's advertisements. The paint was getting quite flaky by then but it always gave me a thrill to think that I had a connection to the club! The Witton End was quite primitive, basically just a long mound of earth with concrete terracing facing the pitch, and no roof or course. The rear slope was uneven and covered in grass. It was around this time too, as I recall, that the club made a share issue and my dad bought 10 shares. I still remember the share certificate pinned to the wall in his office, typed in claret on blue paper.

I remained a Witton Ender until the stand was closed for the building of the North Stand, when I decamped to the Holte End. I would stand near the front, just in front of a crash barrier (if you stood behind you risked getting crushed), on the Trinity Road side of the stand. A school friend and his dad were season ticket holders and they sat in the upper tier of Trinity Road, and I remember waving to them from my spot.

I gave up going to watch football around 1980, having been fairly regular for over a decade. Sadly time has dimmed my memory and I don't really recall many games. I had become disillusioned with football, and remember leaving my last ever match before the end. The match was dismal, Villa were losing, it was raining and finding myself cold, wet and bored I left never to return.

I met this guy at work, at DTI as it was known then, and he was writing a book on all the Irish players in the League at the time. He already had a book published on Manchester United, so we were very excited when he managed to get press passes for the Crystal Palace v Manchester United game, in December 1991. He was a member of some writers' organisation or other, and when he saw how helpful the people at Selhurst were, we went back for two more games; Wimbledon v Chelsea, and the Villa game. I thought it would all lead to something perhaps but we never went back again, and I am not sure if he ever finished his book. The photos were all

on slide, and I had never taken pitch side ones before. I had got the hang of it by the last match, and used a a very flexible Fuji-chrome film, but I was so embarrassed by my kit, which even at that time, was quite outdated. The lens I used cost £30 second hand and was rubbish compared to the huge ones the pros were using, but I was quite pleased with the shots I got.
Gerry Naughton, Harlesdon, North London.

Around 1934 or 1935 I was a teenager of 18 ish and was invited to a dance at a hotel in Birmingham (High Street, I believe near the end of New Street). Pongo Waring was there and he asked me to dance, I was of course delighted. I was a slim 5ft 6in, so he towered above me, and I think his arms would have gone around me twice! I couldn't wait to tell my dad when I got home because he was a staunch Villa supporter who had played for Aston schoolboys on Villa's Perry Barr ground before they moved to Villa Park. I now have two sons and four granddaughters supporting Aston Villa, one of whom played for Villa girls.
Edna Dore, Birmingham.

When we were in the Third Division we had a contact at the club so we always knew where the team would be before the game. We did not talk to the players, we kept our distance for obvious reasons, but they must have thought, 'who are these guys that keep appearing before and after games?' We were in a pub on the way to Reading, and I learned that Andy Lochhead was doubtful for the game. I was in the loo when in came Andy for a pee next to me. I couldn't resist it. 'Are you playing today Andy?' 'Yes' was the reply. 'Great', I said and rushed back to my pals with the news. At the ground we assured fellow fans Andy was in, but we didn't say how we knew. We won (I think 5–2 but would have to check).

We stopped at the pub on the way home and the players were in great form having drinks at the bar. Willie Anderson looked over to us and put his thumb up. They probably got to know our faces but I think they appreciated we didn't pester them in any way.
Robert Dore, Ettington, Stratford-Upon-Avon, Warwickshire.

No player has divided the opinion of Villa fans during the Premier League years more than Savo Milosevic. To some fans he was a hero. To others he was a waste of space. To some he was a very gifted footballer that was ahead of his time. To others he was nothing but pure clumsy. The truth probably lies somewhere in between. Savo was most definitely a hero when he scored an absolute scorcher against Leeds United in the 1996 League Cup Final.

A couple of months after arriving at Villa from Partizan Belgrade (based on the evidence of a video tape), he raced from one end of the pitch to the other end of the pitch were the Villa fans were sitting in the Darwin End at

Blackburn when he scored his first goal for the club. Less than two years later though his Villa days were numbered when an infamous spitting incident at that same ground.

Whatever your opinions of the Serbian he was certainly value for money when Brian Little splashed out £3.5 million in the summer of 1995. While he never looked like he would recreate his goalscoring that he produced in his homeland he still averaged a goal every three games with 33 goals in 117 appearances. And when he wasn't in the team it was noticed, as Dwight Yorke often scored more goals when Milosevic was in the side.

We should also never forget that the club made a bit of interest when he was sold to Spanish outfit Real Zaragoza for £3.7 million.

Stuart, Birmingham.
www.astonvilla.vitalfootball.co.uk

Paul Birch began his career in the Aston Villa youth system, becoming a regular first-team player in the 1983–84 season after making his League debut in August 1983. His first-team debut had come earlier that year when he replaced Gary Shaw for the final 12 minutes of the European Super Cup victory at home to Barcelona.

During the 1980s he was the mainstay of the Villa midfield – able to play on the right or in the centre – and through his tenacious performances became a firm Holte End favourite.

Sadly, Paul passed away at the tender age of 46 on 2 February 2009 at the Good Hope Hospital in Sutton Coldfield after suffering from bone cancer for some time. 'The Paul Birch Trust' was later set up and run by the Aston Villa Former Players Association (AVFPA) with the aim of ensuring a better quality of life for his 10-year-old daughter.

One of his close friends, Charlie Singh, talks with great affection about the short time he knew Paul.

I was introduced to Paul when he came to my warehouse and we bumped into each other, had a chat and we soon became very good friends. That was only about six or seven years ago but we soon became very close mates. He was a man very dear to everyone's hearts, a lovely, beautiful human being, a fantastic fella. It's very difficult to explain how Paul was; he was just a simple, lovely, loving lad. You only had to be in his company for five minutes to love him. God bless him.

We used to call him 'Pluggy' and we used to go and drink up the 'Jinglers' as we called it – The Crown and Anchor in West Bromwich or in The Sportsmans Club in West Bromwich where we had some fantastic times.

I used to go and watch him play for the Aston Villa Old Stars. I remember Tony Morley saying to me, 'When your little mate "Birchy" is playing this one-two touch football, you can't live with him.' Tony was right. He was a super player – just one or two touches is all he needed. Nobody will ever forget the day he marked the great German midfielder Lothar Matthäus out of the game in a UEFA Cup match at Villa Park against Inter Milan. The World Footballer of the Year couldn't get anywhere near little 'Birchy'.

Charlie Singh, Sutton Coldfield, West Midlands.

I first met Paul Birch in the Jewellery Quarter in Birmingham some years ago while I was doing some business there and we remained friends until he sadly passed away.

Paul Birch was a smashing lad. He never talked about anyone, never had a bad name to say about anyone. I remember about five years ago, we played football on the beach at Benalmadena near Malaga. I went in goal, which was not the best position to play as we had all been in the pub all day and we were all worse for the booze. Birchy was on my side but it didn't help much as the other team scored six goals from six shots past me. Birchy was floating some good balls into the box but we couldn't score. I must have looked a sight as I was wearing brand new brogues on the beach.

In the morning, we were walking down the front at Benalmadena (all 10 of us) and we decided to have a cup of coffee so we found this Irish bar. Anyway, we never did have that coffee but we had a bottle of beer instead. This bar had a 'bookies' in it and we went in there at 10am with only about 5 Euros each, which we put into a 'kitty' but we left the bar at 1am the next day with 800 Euros; we never stopped winning. During that time, we ended up having lunch, dinner and supper in that bar, while we were drinking

Paul Birch with Tamworth's own Mr Manchester United, Barry Baxter, pictured at Bolehall Swifts FC c.1991.

and backing the horses. After we left the bar we then piled into a night club but we soon ran out of money following the day's eating, drinking and gambling. Birchy, who liked his horse racing, even picked a winner at 10/1.

Birchy was also a good snooker player. He was one of the guys who was good at most sports. I thought I was a decent snooker player, but when I played him he would absolutely slaughter me. He must have practised alot on his own snooker table at home to be that good.

Later on Paul would come to my house and I'd go to his house and we had many a good time together. He did some presentation evenings at Bolehall Swifts FC where I was (and still am) Chairman. He was a lovely lad and never refused to attend the evenings at the club. He would always speak to anyone and give autographs and never upset anyone. I liked him that much that I even went to watch him play when he went to play for the Wolves.

Geoff Mulvey, Chairman of Bolehall Swifts FC, Tamworth, Staffordshire.
www.clubwebsite.co.uk/bolehallswiftsfc

In the 1930s, my father had a butchers shop 300 yards from the Villa ground in Church Lane, Aston until it got bombed during the War. In 1936, dad took me to my first game and we stood in the Witton Lane stand. I will always remember a couple of characters we always saw at every home match. There was one chap who only had one leg and he used to strap on his artificial leg over his trousers and he then started to run round the running track before the game for a laugh. The whole ground clapped him as he ran round the pitch.

Another character I remember, he must have been about 60 years old, he used to wear the same old dirty rain coat and flat cap and he used to run onto the pitch before the game, throw his cap onto the pitch and dribble it towards the goal and shoot his cap into the net. Each time he did this he'd receive a standing ovation from the crowd.

The first goalkeeper I ever saw at Villa Park was Biddlestone, then there was Rutherford and Wakeman. I also remember outfield players like Frank Broome, Harry Parkes and George Cummings. After training days, they all used to go in the same old dirty café we frequented as kids, which was situated just round the corner from Villa Park. As a kid, I remember I used to fetch the tea for the players and we would have a chat to them. In them days, the players trained at the gym in the Trinity Road stand. You couldn't call it training, more like a few exercises.

My favourite player of all time was George Cummings from the 1940s. He was a left back and he was uncanny. He would stand just a couple of yards off the goal-line and when the ball came over to him, he'd actually back heel the ball over his head before the ball went over the line. I saw him do that a few times. I also seem to remember that Eric Houghton once had the hardest shot in football. Even with the heavy leather ball, which was even heavier when it was soaking wet, his shot rifled through the air like a cannon ball. As for the boots, they were like steel.

If I'm not mistaken, Stan Lynn scored 10 goals from full-back in the 1957–58 season under Houghton. He scored most of them when the winger would take a short corner which he passed to Stan Lynn and he would rifle it into the net.

The most extraordinary goal I ever saw was when full-back Peter Aldis scored a header from the halfway line. Yes, the halfway line. He was in the right-back position and saw the goalkeeper way off his line and he headed the ball from just on the half way line and it flew over the 'keeper into the empty net. Aldis must have had a headache after that!!

As kids, I can remember we used to roll down the grass bank at the Witton End, years before it was developed. When I got home, filthy dirty from rolling down the muddy grass bank, I'd have a tin bath waiting for me in front of the fire. The bath was always cold because my mother used to tell me, 'come home like that again and you'll have a cold bath.'

Something that I will always treasure is a 1957 FA Cup scarf which my wife bought in Covent Garden before the game. I later got it signed by Peter McParland himself. It was actually featured recently in the *Aston Villa News & Record*.

In the 1950s, my wife and I had a 1934 Austin Seven, among others, and we used to go all over the country to watch the Villa in it. We always said that if the car ever broke down en route to a match we would sell it for scrap wherever we were and come back home by some other mode of transport. There was one time when we were travelling back from Highbury and we were driving along the old M1 and the wheel arch collapsed and the car rested on top of the tyre, so we suddenly ground to a halt. As we got out, the tyre lifted off the wheel so I told my wife to go and sit in the rear passenger seat and I went to sit in the front passenger seat in order to release the wheel arch off the wheel. Here I was, a 6ft 4in man driving a car from the passenger seat all the way from Daventry back to Birmingham.

I never miss a home game to this day. As someone who is disabled, the club look after me. I arrive at the reception at 11am and have a cup of tea with the girls on the reception desk. All the former players who pass through the reception come and speak to me. Not long ago, the club gave me and my wife use of a box for six games. My wife was ill a couple of years ago and she had a card from Martin O'Neill when she was in hospital. Not only that Ken McNaught came to the hospital to see my wife. Unfortunately, my wife died in April 2010 and there was an article in the *Birmingham Mail*, **'Villa wonderfan dies age 78'**. There was another full page article in the paper about the 'perk' the club gave me – the parking space which used to belong to Doug Ellis outside the North Stand Reception. I regularly correspond with Mr Lerner and General Krulak.

All these old timers talk about football being better in the 1940s and 1950s but I disagree. Football now is fast, more technical and tactical and players get paid huge wages but in my day, footballers were on a 'tenner' a week. Recently, I spoke to Peter McParland who went to see Villa play Tottenham at White Hart Lane with Pat Jennings. He told me that he lived in the same street in Ireland as Pat Jennings and when he came out of the ground at the end of the game, he saw a yellow Porsche in the players' car park. He said to Jennings, 'It must be fantastic to have the money to buy a car like that?' Jennings replied by saying, 'Yeah, he's got four like that.' How times have changed?

Ivor Price, Erdington, Birmingham.

I was a member of the Travellers Club when Charlie Taverner was in charge of the Lions Club. We used to go to various away games with the Travellers Club. On one particular trip we were coming back down the M6 from the North (it may have been Blackpool), when the coach driver announced over the PA system that a Flights coach had pulled up in the lay-by ahead of us and we were going to pull up behind it. As we pulled over into the lay-by, we noticed it was the Villa team coach. The players on the Flights coach were waiting to be picked up by another coach. Our coach driver asked us if we minded sharing the coach with the players. Obviously, we all agreed to this and shortly after the players climbed aboard our coach.

So, we carried on our journey, sharing seats with the Villa first team players and staff. We were sat in front of Brian Godfrey and Brian Tyler and talking to them about the game, as if they were just fans like us. They were very nice people. It was like a dream come true at the time having all the players sitting on your coach. I remember Dick Edwards was on the coach and he had his guitar with him and on the way back to Birmingham he decided to get off at somewhere about 60 miles from Birmingham. That was another good memory which stuck in my mind and seeing Dick Edwards with his guitar topped the day.

Years ago, I used to stand in the Witton End with Steven Hunt's mother, Joan. Even when it poured down with rain I remember we ran down the banks at the back of the stand after the final whistle blew. Steven was born in Witton and was surprisingly turned down as a youngster with Villa. I worked with his mother at the GEC in Witton and one of the foremen in the factory at the time was Vic Crowe's father-in-law. So one day we went over to Vic Crowe's father-in-law and we told him that Steve Hunt should be given a game. As it turned out, he got in touch with Vic Crowe and eventually made seven appearances for the first team in the early 1970s.

Fred Hubball, Curdworth, Sutton Coldfield, West Midlands.

My company, T. Sabeker, was formed in 1903 and were originally based in Aston Brook Street then moved to Phillips Street, Aston. We were a brass foundry but later became a shop fitting company. Eventually, I became Vice-Chairman of the company about nine or 10 years ago. Some time ago, I was looking at some minutes from a meeting held around 1905 and it stated that there was a meeting with a Mr William McGregor, who was Villa Chairman at the time and they talked about football. This told me that even in those early days. Mr McGregor was keen to get local businessmen on board with his ideas.

Mike Sabeker, Wishaw, Sutton Coldfield, West Midlands.

When I was about six years old I used to watch Grandstand with my dad, who was not really a football fan, more a racing man but when the football results came through I always thought the name 'Aston Villa' was a really cool name. So that's where my allegiance to Villa began. Even though they were awful and languishing at the lower half of the division, I liked the name. However, I stuck by them even though all my school mates teased me all the time about supporting such a rubbish team (well, we were then). In those days, I didn't go to the matches, just followed their results on TV.

One of the first names I remember was Derek Dougan and particularly watching the results coming through when we played Leicester City in April 1962 and we won 8–3, with Dougan scoring a brace. From that day on, I was hooked. However, I didn't actually go to Villa Park until I was 12 years old. It was against Manchester United and I went along with a couple of United supporters. These were the days of Best, Law and Charlton and United were top of the League (nothing changes there). We were bottom!! It was around 1966–67 and we won 2–1. The game really got me hooked. Winning against the 'Mighty Reds', even when we were rubbish. That was the highlight of the season as we were relegated to Division Two. The next season, I started going a lot. The crowds in that season plummeted to as low as 12,000. Tommy Cummings was manager and Doug Ellis became Chairman for the first time. Times were desperate. Cummings didn't last long and became Doug's first sacking and enter Tommy Docherty. I remember Docherty pleading with the fans for their support through the media and only a month after being appointed, there were over 20,000 to see us win against Norwich and on Boxing Day, 41,000 turned up to see us beat Cardiff.

The game that really sold it to me was when Villa played Southampton in the early rounds of the FA Cup. There was a replay at Villa Park, at night, and there were 59,000 Villa fans (I don't remember seeing any Saints fans) to see us through to the next round. To this day, I have never witnessed an atmosphere like that. The noise was deafening. I think the fans were venting their frustrations for the last few dismal seasons and suddenly, they were seeing their team win a few games.

After that game, I realised how big a club Aston Villa was. At that age I thought we were a 'middle of the road' club. Even when we went down to the Third Division the crowds weren't bad so I thought this must be a big club. I don't know what it was about Villa that I started to become a serious fan; the cool name; the ground; the tradition, I don't know but to me it meant more than my mates who chose to support Manchester United or Liverpool (because they won things) or local clubs like Coventry City or Leicester City.

Another game which sticks out in my memory for me was during the 1976–77 season when Liverpool won the League. A home game against the previous season's Champions and we had arguably the best strike force ever to wear the claret and blue in Gray, Little and Deehan. They were battering teams at Villa Park before the arrival of Liverpool and we ended up beating them 5–1 in a famous victory. It was a night game and I unfortunately missed it. In those days, there was no Sky Sports News so I had to sit at home watching some rubbish on TV. At 9pm the Midlands news came on and they announced the latest score of Aston Villa 5 Liverpool 1. It was 5–1 at half-time and there was still half an hour to play. I couldn't believe it.

Now I'm a father, I even got my son to become a Villa fan and he's an absolute fanatic. More recently, before the home game against Fulham in 2011, I saw these two old chaps walking around the perimeter of the ground. As they walked into the Holte End they both came and sat down randomly, two rows behind us. One of the chaps was none other than Doug Ellis. I thought 'what's he doing in the Holte? He's not going to the bar so where's he going?' Nobody gave them any grief and one or two people were chatting to him. He remained in his seat throughout the game. At

Spot the mystery fan? Doug Ellis sat among the Holte End faithful during the Fulham game in 2010.

half-time, I went to the toilet and came back to find my son had climbed over two sets of seats and was having his picture taken with him. I thought about five or 10 years ago he wouldn't have been able to do that. I actually admire Doug Ellis for what he did for the club.
Ian Robinson, Rugby, Warwickshire.

I remember it was a glorious, sunny Easter Saturday in 1982 when I took my sister to the Villa to see them play Brighton. It was 0–0 at half-time, but we seemed to come to life in the second half with three goals from Geddis (2) and Evans. Apart from the goals, I remember more about incidents after the game more than anything else.

We headed out of the ground following another home win and walked down Witton Lane towards the station. There were alot of Brighton supporters also heading in the same direction and lots of police around monitoring any possible trouble. I was walking in front of my sister and as I turned round to see where she was, I noticed she had disappeared. I stopped and looked around the crowds walking in the same direction, but couldn't see her anywhere. So, I went back and told a policeman in a van that I had lost my sister. I gave him a description of her and he asked me who she supported so I told the policeman she was a Villa fan. He recognised the description of the lady and said, 'Oh dear, in that case we'd better get her out of the van, then.' The copper then turned to my sister and shouted, 'Ida, you'd better come, your brother's found you.' As it turned out, the police thought she was a Brighton fan as she was not wearing any colours (as her scarf had been grabbed off her by a fan) and took her in for her own safety and thought she was from the South and a Brighton troublemaker. Apparently, there was a bit of trouble after the game and she had got innocently caught up in the middle of it. The police did apologise for the mistaken identity and within a week my sister received a written apology from West Midlands Police.
Fred McGreggor, Rugby, Warwickshire.

I played against the Villa Old Stars in 1992 for my club Wake Green Amateurs when Bobby Thomson played. He had a bit of a punch up (nothing unusual there) with our goalie Pete Greenhill. After the match Johnny Dixon came in and apologised, the gentleman he was, and said they never told Bobby about these games but he kept turning up with his boots. Next minute a white handkerchief appeared around the dressing room door, and it was Bobby apologising too. The match ended 2–2, and I remember standing behind Peter Withe who thundered in a header from Bobby's corner to equalise. Only time I've been happy when letting in a goal when playing – to see him rise like a salmon and hammer into the net in vintage style. All the players spent the afternoon in our bar for several hours and we had a great day.
John Hatfield, Treasurer of Wake Green AFC, Moseley, Birmingham.

I met Nigel Callaghan (Aston Villa 1989–1992) in Corfu. When he found out I was a Villa fan he cursed and almost refused to speak to me. He said he hated the Villa from his time there and blamed Doug Ellis for kicking him out of the club and taking his club car off him out of the blue one day at training!! He soon warmed to me when I told him I was at his League debut same day as Ian Ormondroyd and had witnessed his debut goal against Sheffield Wednesday, I think at the Holte End.

Chris Sutton, Birmingham.

I went along on 29 April 1961 to Villa Park in my schoolboy days to see the last game of that season against Sheffield Wednesday. It was a sentimental moment as it was Johnny Dixon's farewell game, Villa thumped Wednesday 4–1 and Johnny even scored. It was a certain Charlie Aitken's debut, but what we did not know was... it would also turn out to be Gerry Hitchens last game in claret and blue. Gerry signed off with a brace and then came the news just two months later that he had moved on to the great Inter Milan, but he left behind a void I've yet to see filled. Now I know how all those old guys on the terraces felt when they talked about Pongo Waring!!

No matter how badly things were going for Villa while we had the GREAT Gerry Hitchens leading our attack I always felt we could turn it round.

Michael L d'Abreu, Birmingham.

My first view of Gerry Hitchens was not of him in a Villa shirt, but in Cardiff City colours in a match at Villa Park towards the end of Villa's FA Cup-winning season of 1957. It was one of those very rare occasions when I went to a match with both my parents, and it was (because of no floodlights at that point) played on a Wednesday afternoon. Villa won easily that day, 4–1, but my father had eyes for the opponent's centre-forward. 'Good player', my dad said afterwards, and I took his word for it, but I was more interested in what the Villa players were doing! However, it was Hitchens that had scored the Cardiff goal!

My dad knew a thing or two about fine footballers. His heyday as a young Villa supporter had been in those starry times at the end of the 1920s and early 1930s, when the Villa, again threatened to take the football world by storm. In those days, there were certain players like Jimmy Gibson, Billy Walker, 'Pongo' Waring and Eric Houghton to admire. He also saw Trevor Ford later on. So, dad had a fair measuring stick to go by.

And so it was that at the end of 1957, Gerry signed for the Villa. That made my dad happy. For me, I was not so sure. This Gerry Hitchens looked alright, but nothing fantastic, I thought. I was not sure what my dad had seen in him. Neither was I sure whether the fact that Gerry was on his

National Service had anything to do with it, after all, a footballer is a footballer, isn't he? What did serving in the Army have to do with things?

But, slowly, Gerry grew on me. And when it came to the decisive match against the West Bromwich Albion in April, 1959 – to decide the relegation issue – Gerry scored the opening goal and until two minutes from the end, Villa looked safe from relegation. It was not Gerry's fault that Villa did go down. He had done his part of the job – in my book at least.

It was that year that Gerry did come into his own, though, with the Army becoming past history. By November 1959, Villa were doing alright in the Second Division, but the Villa forwards were not setting the world alight with their goalscoring. Joe Mercer (Villa's manager) put pressure on his men by threatening he would play the reserves if they didn't start hitting the net more often. The result was startling – 11 goals were scored against Charlton Athletic! Gerry scored five of those, the last breaking the poor keeper's finger as he tried to save it!

The magnificent goalscoring didn't end there. Villa then scored five at Bristol City (Gerry grabbing another three), and then five more at home against Scunthorpe with Gerry getting two more, to make his tally for those three consecutive matches a lovely 10 goals! Villa got promotion that season, and Gerry and Peter McParland finished with 25 goals apiece.

The next season (1960–61) proved to be the pinnacle year for Gerry in England. At one point he was regularly scoring two goals a week, and finished with 29 League goals and 42 goals overall. Apart from his hat-trick against our cross-city neighbours, Birmingham City, my most vivid memory of him in his last season – reflecting both his determination and confidence – was in a home match against Blackpool (31 December 1960). Then Blackpool were a club not yet on the wane, still having a player of the class of Jimmy Armfield, then England's regular right-back. It was Gerry who pursued Armfield to the by-line, stole the ball off him and after moving closer to goal hit a stunning shot from an angle of no more than 30 degrees and a distance of 18 yards. I was virtually right behind that shot, and I saw the ball hit the back of the net off the far upright before you could blink! And that with a heavy leather ball!

The final Villa game of the 1960–61 season (and indeed Gerry's final game for Villa) was against League runners-up Sheffield Wednesday (29 April 1961) and England goalkeeper Ron Springett. Villa won 4–1. Villa brought back the old Cup-winning legendary skipper, Johnny Dixon, for his last match, and the *Birmingham Post* headline read: 'Hitchens Finds a Foil – Too Late', clearly indicating the degree of Dixon's help to Hitchens (who scored two, the first – early in the match – from an adept Dixon assist). It was extraordinary that Villa's old skipper and Hitchens played their last match that day for the Villa. Both looked like supreme strikers, and we would have loved it if they could have continued in that partnership.

Gerry Hitchens won his first England cap while still a Villa player against Mexico, which England won 8–0. He scored the first goal in the first minute or two and played in an England team that contained the likes of Johnny Haynes, Bobby Charlton and Bobby Robson. He didn't look out of place in that company.

Not long after came the news that Inter Milan had signed Gerry. It was a hammer-blow for the supporters, and even though Tony Hateley eventually came and showed his great scoring skills, it was never going to be the same without Gerry. And, as Villa languished in the lower reaches of the Football League some ten years later, the rumour started that Hitchens was coming back to England from Italy, and that he might re-sign for the Villa. The thought of that was akin to the news of King Richard returning from the Holy Land to return to his subjects, but, alas, it was not to be.

And, of course, the announcement of his premature death in 1983 was a great shock to me and every Villa fan!

If Gerry Hitchens was not the best centre-forward Villa have ever had, then all I can say is that he must have been very close to that standard. An unselfish player, he remains the Villa's most regular goal scorer since the War, and his cowboy-like style when he was on the scoring warpath was a sight to be seen.

John Lerwill, Hodge Hill, Birmingham.

My first Villa match was in 1947. Aston Villa v Brentford and we won 2–0. I was also at the historic Villa v Manchester United game when we lost 6–4 in 1948 with some Villa greats playing including Trevor Ford, Frank Moss, Joe Rutherford, Leslie Smith, George Edwards, George Cummings, etc. I have also seen the Villa at Wembley, never in the FA Cup but the League Cup. I was there when we lost to Spurs, also when we beat Manchester United and two years later against Leeds United. During a period of madness I also went by coach to Sweden ten years ago (or more) to see us beaten but enjoyed every moment of the nightmare journey there and back.

I must confess at the onset that I did play football (right-half) and I did sign forms for Birmingham City - but don't tell anyone!

Stephen Morris, Aspiran, Herault, South of France.

Aston Villa player Tommy Ball was murdered on 11 November 1923. He was shot dead by his next door neighbour and landlord George Stagg after an argument with him in his back garden. Yes, that was in 1923! Tommy was a great centre-half and had played 77 times for Villa. It has been said that he had been the only professional footballer to have been murdered. Tommy, aged just 23 had lived in Somerville Cottages, Brick-Kiln Lane (now re-named Beeches Road) in Perry Barr, north Birmingham. Tommy and his wife Beatrice had spent about an hour of the evening of 11 November in their local pub, The Church Tavern in Church Lane (now Church Road),

Villa player Tommy Ball was murdered on 11 November 1923. Here is his grave stone which is in Perry Barr, Birmingham.

Perry Barr. It was on their return to their home that evening that the tragedy happened.

Tommy was buried just yards away from The Church Tavern at St John's Church, Perry Barr. Hundreds of people lined the streets watching the cortege making its way to the church.

My interest into the investigation into Tommy Ball's life and death began when I saw a picture of him in the corridors of the North Stand at Villa Park, I was intrigued and fascinated why and the way in which such a young talented footballer should have been murdered. I read the only book I could find on the subject by Paul Lester called *The Murder of Tommy Ball; An Aston Villa Tragedy.* I then began to try and trace some of the places that Tommy would have known around Aston in the short time he spent here. I was also shocked to find how his grave had once been left in such a state of neglect and desecration and that many Villa fans were still unaware of who Tommy Ball was and what had happened to him. I still feel that this is the case and I have been keen in trying to make not just Villa fans but football fans everywhere aware of his life by putting out the information of his life and death with photos out onto the Internet.

Simon Hayward, Tamworth, Staffordshire.

In about 1958 my neighbour and I, Lily Summers, and my dad, Billy Summers, were on our way to the Villa ground. On passing a bus stop we noticed two Aston Villa players Jackie Sewell and Jimmy Dugdale waiting for the bus to get to the match to play. We stopped and offered them a lift to the game and managed to squash them in the back seat of a 1950s Ford Popular. From then onwards I remember at away games we always looked out for Villa players and they used to give us free tickets to watch the matches in the stands.

The first time I went down the Villa I was 14 years old (in 1955) I went to see Villa against Blackpool and the score was 1–1 and it was Sir Stanley Matthews's birthday on that day.

I have had a season ticket on and off since 1957 in the Trinity Road. I was also there at the 11–1 match against Charlton in 1959, and there was only a small crowd about 18,000.

Peter McParland book signing 1961 at Lewis's in Birmingham. The youngster standing next to the security guard is Gordon Brown from Sheldon (aged 12), wearing the white coat. Mr McParland was actually speaking to me at the time. I was unaware and nearly never said hello back.

Early in 1961 I was asked by my mother to visit a relative, but as a youngster I had other ideas. Not only a soccer legend but a hero of mine was doing a book signing in a large store called Lewis's. The player was Peter McParland, so off to the store I went and managed to get to the front of the crowd. At Christmas time in 1961 I was 12 years old and I was given a football annual called 'All Stars'. There was a card in the book marking a page where there was a photograph of Peter McParland signing the book with me at the front of the crowd. It was then I came clean to my mother that I actually went elsewhere and not the errand I was asked to do. Needless to say I got a right ear bashing from mum.

Gordon Brown, Sheldon, Birmingham.

My nan gave me a Villa scarf in 1992 which she obtained from collecting the wrappers on mushy peas tins, saved them up and sent off for it. It was a generic Villa/West Ham type bar scarf. Around 2006 I decided to sew our badge when we won the European Cup and it just went on from there really, collecting badges and sewing them onto my scarf. Now the badges appear on both sides but unfortunately there's no room left on the scarf. There's around 70 unique badges. I have cut them off old playing shirts, bought them off Ebay, the rare ones like those made by Coffer Sports, and friends kindly donated them to me.

Darren Cassin, Ward End, Birmingham.

Darren Cassin outside Villa Park holding up his Villa scarf.

Claret and Blue Awaydays

Maybe you are one of those fans who is sick of giving money to his or her own club, but still wants to go to games or maybe you are one of the committed few who will willingly get up at 5am to travel the length of the country on a regular basis (or Europe) to see the team get hammered 6–1 and then not get home until gone midnight. Maybe you have noticed that the away fans generally seem to be singing louder, jumping about more, and just generally having more fun. The reasons are plentiful, but there comes a time in almost every football fan's life that they decide, 'I want to go to an away game.'

From my own experience, this is somewhat true as it seemed too often that Villa's away support had always been better, by and large, than the home support. I can look back at Highbury in May 1981 when I was among the 25,000 Villa fans witnessing history in the making. I've never known support like it and we lost the game! I also remember standing watching a dreadful Villa performance at Prenton Park in the semi-final of the League Cup in 1994, but hopes were raised when Dalian Atkinson hit home a consolation goal which would prove invaluable. Then there were the four or five trips to Wembley when our support was nothing short of incredible.

In this chapter, a selection of Villa fans have written their own accounts of some away games they attended in the past; some good experiences, some not so good; some remembered with fondness, some not. All in all, I hope you enjoy reading them and maybe you will remember going to a few?

☸

Selhurst Park   3 October 1992
Wimbledon 2 Villa 3

The Villa team of the 1992–93 season produced some incredible football, and for one glorious half season the undoubted star of that team was Dalian Atkinson. Blessed with pace, power and an almost feline grace, when Atkinson was in the mood, he was close to unstoppable. There were a string of magnificent performances before injury ruled him out for a while but when he came back for the run-in, his return should have given the impetus for the final push but nothing about Dalian was ever predictable and instead he merely disrupted the team.

Do you remember that memorable match when Dalian Atkinson ran more than half the length of the Selhurst Park pitch on a wet Saturday afternoon in October 1992 and left opponent after opponent in his wake before chipping the ball over the stranded 'keeper? The wonder goal was

Dean Saunders jumps on Dalian Atkinson's back after scoring a wonder goal in 1992. 'Rainman' Martin Pritchard looks on with his 'brolly'.

voted Goal of the Season for 1992 by the Match of the Day viewers and helped Villa beat the 'Wombles' 3–2, with Atkinson scoring the winner.

However, can you recall 'what happened next' as Atkinson ran towards the Villa fans behind the goal? Well, Dean Saunders leapt on Dalian's back before a supporter stepped forward and handed them an umbrella. The next day, that picture was splashed all over the Sunday papers, but whatever happened to that supporter (and the brolly)?

That man was Martin Pritchard from Stourbridge, a life long Villa fan who travelled down to Selhurst Park just after having an operation on his ankle and with his 'brolly' in tow.

That day I took a stool to Selhurst Park because I had a long term problem with my ankle so the steward found me a place right at the front of the stand, behind the goal and right next to the pitch. It was the first time I had been that close to the pitch. I was sat on the stool watching the game and all I remember was it was pouring with rain. I had my 'brolly' up for most of the game; it was actually the first time I had taken a 'brolly' to a game. Then, I remember I was so excited when Dalian Atkinson scored this fantastic goal and in one of those spur of the moment thoughts, I leapt off my stool and ran onto the pitch, with my 'brolly' in tow. The next thing I knew Dean Saunders was jumping on Dalian Atkinson's back right next to me so I distinctively held my 'brolly' up over them. I didn't know what I was doing; I couldn't believe it. If I remember rightly, Dalian didn't say anything to me. All I remember was that I thought I had to get off the pitch before I got arrested. As I walked off the pitch, one of the stewards said, 'come on, you'd better come back into the stand.'

The next day, my picture was in all the Sunday papers and I was even on *Match of the Day!* Since that day, whenever I've been abroad with Villa and other supporters have realised who I am, people have asked to have their photo taken with me. I still have a tee-shirt with that famous picture on and the question, 'Who are yer..?' and a list of European venues I have visited as a Villa fan, accompanied by the words, 'Rainman on tour'.

In 2002, a decade on, I wrote to the Villa and told them the story and they invited me to Villa Park to have my picture taken on the pitch. I was featured in the *Aston Villa News & Record* for the game against Leeds United on 6 October 2002, almost 10 years to the day.

Little did I know that Dalian's goal was later voted *Match of the Day's* Goal of the Season for 1992 and every time they show it, I'm on the film.
Martin Pritchard (aka 'The Rainman'), Stourbridge, West Midlands.

St Andrews   12 December 1987
Birmingham City 1 Villa 2

I will always remember going to St Andrews in 1987 and watching Garry Thompson score the two goals to win the game for us. I was about 13 years of age and remember walking up to St Andrews and was amazed at the state of the place, thinking 'is this really a football ground?' You had to walk up a grass bank to get to the ground. I thought this is more like a park than a football stadium. When I approached the ground, I recall a mass of Villa fans all trying to get in (in the days before all ticket games). Only being small and slight in stature, I was getting crushed by the herds of fans trying to get in. Then I saw a policeman on horseback approaching me and all of a sudden he lifted me up by the scruff of the neck and dropped me at the front of the queue so I could just walk through the turnstile to get in.

This was my first away game and being used to going to Villa Park, I was appalled by the state of St Andrews. It was pretty dire compared to our ground. How the other half live, eh? Looking round the ground, I could see one section of the ground had been closed off and I saw Villa fans climbing in one end and Blues fans climbing in at the other and they met in the middle and a mass scrap started (well it was at the time when soccer violence was at its peak). For a 13 year-old, this was pretty frightening to say the least. While I was watching this happen in front of me I saw this big Blues fan, a skinhead and dressed in denim, get arrested. This guy looked about 6ft 8in tall to me, even though he was only about 5ft 9in or something like that, but he seemed huge to me. As he was being escorted past the Villa fans I started calling him some names, being the cheeky 13-year-old I was then. To my amazement, he managed to get loose from the police and ran up to the 7ft fence, segregating the sections of the ground. As he approached the fence, I ran away. All the other Villa fans around me saw this and laughed. I heard some say, 'kid he can't get you from there.' After watching Garry Thompson score the two goals to seal the win, I was glad to get home from the 'war zone' back to North Birmingham – alive!!
Danny Drewry, Sutton Coldfield, West Midlands.
www.MidlandsMemorabilia.com

Villa's pre-season tour of Switzerland, 1989
I don't tend to remember anything about the games I've been to as it's usually about the day out or the few days away if it's a European match or a pre-season tour. The pre-season for me is always the best part of the year, especially when you've got a little trip abroad as you can combine the football with a mini-holiday with your mates. If you're single (as I was in the late 1980s), there was the added advantage of pulling a few women.

My first pre-season tour was in 1989 when I went to Switzerland with four or five mates (two of them I still go to home and away games with 22 years later). It was a great trip for many reasons, some I can't talk about but one being because we visited some beautiful places and met some nice people. I have always travelled but in 1989, it was something new for me to travel abroad to watch Villa play. When we arrived at Zurich Airport we bumped into our new signing at the time, Kent Nielson, who thought I was part of the club, but I told him 'I was just a fan'.

The first game was against Servette Geneva. The game was not in the beautiful city, but it was played miles away in a really small village which we couldn't find on four different maps but we eventually got there. The pitch was laid on top of a nuclear bunker and we lost that game if I remember rightly, without manager Graham Taylor, who was back home making some summer signings.

Next up was a game against a combined team. We based ourselves in Basel, even though the game was not played there. Again, we lost the game against a bunch of part-timers but the only thing I remember was we had a really good time, before, during and after the match. I do remember the hotel we checked into though. It was a very basic hotel, clean and tidy and run by a couple of gay fellas, which didn't bother us as it was really cheap. However, when we came down for a drink in the bar at night, it was full of 'ladies of the night.' It was only at that point we found that the hotel was in fact nothing more than a 'knocking shop'. However, I decided not to use my room that particular night, even though I had paid for it, because I had met a nice young lady from Manchester (way before I was married, might I add).

To prove it was not all beer, women and football, we did a fair amount of sightseeing in between games. We travelled down to Zermatt, where Switzerland's most famous mountain (The Matterhorn) can be found and spent the night there. In our third game, we moved on to a place called Winterthur. Villa drew that game 4–4 to continue the disappointing run of results and that was followed by another good night out on the town.

For the fifth game we travelled to a place called Solothurn in the north of Switzerland. We went to the Tourist Information office and managed to find a really cheap hotel there but little did we know it was where the Villa were staying throughout their tour (no expenses spared in those days). Villa finally won the game against Solothurn by 6–0, including a Dean Spink hat-trick. The travelling fans were in full song for that game. Just as well, because I noticed a chap filming the game with a video recorder. I had a word with him and asked him if I could have a copy when he got it home. So, I gave him my name and address and thought nothing more of it, thinking I'd never see the copy of the game.

Anyway, we moved on again for the last game of the tour to a town called Echallens near Lausanne which is situated near Lake Geneva. This left me in a bit of a pickle as I needed to get back to Zurich, which was further north, after the game. We won that game 8–0 on a very sunny day. Straight after the game and a few beers later, I decided to hitchhike my way to the local tram station. I was lucky enough to get a lift with a young French lady who spoke little English, and I spoke no French but we had a jolly good conversation for the next 20 minutes in pigeon English and pigeon French all the way to the train station. I needed to get the train back to Zurich but by now I had run out of money apart from about 20 Swiss francs, which wouldn't last long as everything was so expensive.

I managed to get on the number seven tram, which I was told was the right tram to where I wanted to get to. I was on the tram and I asked a couple how many stops before so-and-so station (can't remember the name of the place I had to get off at). Everyone started laughing. 'What's so funny?' I asked. 'You're going the wrong way.' The couple replied. I shrugged it off and thought, no problem I'll just jump off and get another one the other way. Then there was more laughter from the couple. I was thinking, 'What have I said so funny this time?' The couple explained that was the last tram of the night. So, I got off in the middle of nowhere, still a bit hung-over, found a nice bit of garden in front of some flats, plonked myself down and spent the night there. Next morning, I woke up to the noise of a car crashing into a wall. Apparently, the driver saw me flaked out in front of the garden looking like Dracula and took his eyes off the road and crashed into a wall. I don't think they had seen anything like me in that town before. Some drunken football fan, miles from where he should have been, flaked out in front of a posh garden.

Not having slept much that night, I checked into the local Youth Hostel for the last night in Switzerland before I had to get back to the UK. By now, I only had 5 Swiss Francs on me but as I walked around the building, Lady Luck must have been on my side that day as I spotted a 20 Franc note on the floor, which I duly grabbed and tucked away in my pocket, thank you very much!!

The next day I was back in London but a few days later, a package arrived out of the blue with a copy of the video from the game in Solothurn. How amazing that chap had remembered to post that video. After that trip I was hooked on pre-season tours because we went on the next three or four tours following Villa, pre-season to places like Sweden and Germany and I still go to most European games with Villa.
Jon Farrelly, Hillingdon, London.

Ayresome Park   27 December 1976
Middlesbrough 3 Villa 2

My Mom and Dad were going up to Middlesbrough for the game in Dad's nice big fancy Datsun he had just bought. I could have gone with them and done the driving but no, I decided to travel up with a mate in my Mini 850 and be independent. Who wants to go anywhere with their parents when you are 19?

As the game was lost at 3–2 we decided to leave early and as I was trying to get out of town I actually found myself behind Dad at the traffic lights. As the lights changed I stalled. 'Bye Dad!' The car wouldn't start and the headlights flickered as I tried to get going. I pulled the choke out (remember them?) to see if that would do the trick. 'Oops!' In my temper I really pulled the choke out, I now found I had a button with a piece of loose cable in my hand!!! That was an added problem as the car wouldn't tick over right before and for a few days I'd been driving with the choke just ever so ever so slightly out, so it did not cut out.

Ok! I got out of the car. We needed to get help. It started to snow, really snow. I found a garage and the guy came out and towed us in, charged us about £30 to charge the battery up and got us going. As long as I drove and kept my foot on the gas a bit at all times it wouldn't cut out I thought.

I sort of improvised by using my other foot to hit the brake. About 30 miles on the headlights started to dim and it dawned on me that the battery was not charging so if I stopped, I wouldn't get it started again. So as long as I drove non-stop back to Birmingham through the snow with the headlights getting dimmer and my foot remained on the gas at all times so it wouldn't cut out we would be ok. In those days there was no fast road from the M1, so I had to negotiate down through Ashby and Measham when I exited the M1 at Castle Donnington.

I nearly made it. I very nearly made it. About two or three miles from home I stalled at a set of traffic lights. After walking through snow drifts in Walmley at two in the morning I got to a phone box and an old man came out to the rescue. When I eventually got home I found out that Mom and Dad got back home at about 8pm. I was not happy! The first thing I said to Dad was, 'That's it Dad, I ain't ever going to an away match again!' Dad replied, 'Calm down, son, you will. You will.'

And I did!

Roger Hatfield, Sutton Coldfield, West Midlands.

Plough Lane   9 January 1991, FA Cup third-round replay

Wimbledon 1 Villa 0

We got as far as North London at around 12.30pm (in the car) and followed the coaches. They got lost around Kew Gardens, then scrambled eventually into roughly the right district but we couldn't find Plough Lane for love nor money! Eventually we parked up and followed a man who looked as though he may have been going to the game (he was, thankfully), greeted by a sign saying £7 to stand. We paid, walked down the steps at 3.05pm to see Garry Thompson score the game's only goal. For them!!

And then 'our kid' went the wrong way round the M25 on the way home!! What a day to forget.

Lee Smith, Birmingham.

Molineux   26 September 2010

Wolverhampton Wanderers 1 Villa 2

After a disappointing start to the season following the resignation of Martin O'Neill, our first West Midlands derby of the season was at Molineux, coincidently it was new manager Gerard Houllier's first match in charge. It was also the first derby I attended with both of my brothers and being Black Country boys it is our big derby. After two draws in the previous campaign following Wolves' return to the Premier League we were keen to get one over our locals. The match itself was exactly the sort of battle teams had come to expect from Wolves under Mick McCarthy, particularly at home. Stewart Downing opened the scoring for Villa, a delicious Marc Albrighton cross putting it on a plate for him to volley home from close range at the back post. In the second half Wolves equalised out of nothing and the game looked to be heading for another draw until the 87th minute. Downing brought the ball over the halfway line and passed down the left hand side to Ashley Young. He then played it first time into Stephen Warnock, who crossed towards the penalty spot for Emile Heskey to bury an unstoppable bullet header low into the bottom corner of the net in front of a silent South Bank. Magic!

Standing on the halfway line I only saw the ball go past the side netting so I was not initially sure it had gone in. A colleague next to me jumped into the air, I asked 'Is it in?' He leapt into my arms screaming 'Yes!!' Bedlam hit. My brothers and I were still celebrating even after Wolves had restarted the game. I've been fortunate enough to witness several late derby winners during my time at the club but that one stands right up there. The much-maligned, yet much under-appreciated Emile Heskey gave me one of my very favourite Aston Villa moments. Cheers Emile!

Mark Jones, Birmingham (Aston Villa employee).

The County Ground   6 October 1970, Football League Cup third round

Northampton Town 1 Villa 1

The worst away game I can ever remember going to was a League Cup game at Northampton in the 1970s. We travelled independently from Rugby to Northampton by train. The game ended up in a draw so we would have to play them again at Villa Park. There were all sorts of trouble during and after the game, one of the worst for violence I have ever witnessed. There were police everywhere and they gave the away fans no protection whatsoever. By the time we got back to the station, sometime after the end of the game, the 'Villa Special' was at the platform waiting to depart for Birmingham. Villa scarves were hanging out of the windows in typical 1970s fashion. As we entered the station a policeman stopped us, seeing we were Villa fans and asked us where we were going and I replied, 'Rugby'. The officer just said, pointing at the 'Villa Special', 'No you're not!! You're not hanging round Northampton. Get back on that train with the rest of the scum.'

We had to go to Birmingham (as the train did not stop anywhere other than New Street) and then catch the last train back to Rugby. We eventually got back to Rugby well after midnight. I think it was a bit like that in those days going to away games was not managed or policed very well, unlike it is today.

Ian Robinson, Rugby, Warwickshire.

Highbury 2 May 1981

Arsenal 2 Villa 0

It turned out to be the best day for years, but for about 45 minutes on 2 May 1981 I can remember feeling sick at the thought of throwing away the League title as Arsenal were cruising in the second half and Ipswich were 1–0 up at Middlesbrough.

In the days before mobile phones, it was the pockets of fans with little portable radios and word spreading across the terrace as 'Boro's goals went in that sticks in the memory.

I can't imagine what the atmosphere would have been like after the game if Ipswich had won!!
Nick Harper, Birmingham.

I travelled up to Highbury from Guildford where I was at university at the time. I made a detour to Euston to meet all the Villa fans off the train but hardly came across any; I thought they must have all come down on coaches? I then managed to get lost in North London trying to find the ground (Highbury), but luckily hitched up with some youngsters who looked about 12 (I was only 18 at the time) who were going to the game. I can't even remember if they were Villa or Arsenal fans, but it didn't matter as long as I got there.

As is typical of Villa we nearly managed to bugger it up. I can still see that McDermott goal crossing the line in slow motion as Jimmy Rimmer looked on as if it was literally yesterday. 30 years ago, good grief! I remember the rumour going round the North Bank; first that Ipswich had scored, then that 'Boro had actually done so...Of course, technically speaking, it was not a rumour that Boro had scored against Ipswich! It just felt like it for about two minutes. Oh and I remember coming round the corner to see a pub with furniture piled up outside it – tables and chairs – and Villa fans all over it singing and dancing.
Richard Moore, Chichester, West Sussex.

It was a surreal day for me and my mates. We got to New St with no travel organised, and Andy Brown's two coaches were 'C Crew' regulars only with the special trains utterly sold out. We were heading down to Digbeth when a 50-year-old Arthur Daley lookalike asked us if we wanted to jump on his coach to London for a fiver. On we jumped, chuffed to bits at our luck.

We were dropped off near the ground to be told by 'Arthur Daley' that the return would only be leaving the Green Man in Edgware Rd at closing time. I was at school in sixth form then and was raiding the piggy bank and working with my father to afford footie and a few pints twice a week, so I

Villa fans gathered behind the goal at the Clock End at Highbury on 2 May 1981.

had just about enough money left for a bag of chips and a can of pop to last me the whole day.

It was very hot and sunny before the game and the pubs and streets near the ground were overflowing with Villa fans. Surprisingly, the (admittedly older) Arsenal fans who spoke to us were pretty friendly and thought we were the best team in the League and told us we would definitely win it. Often neglected in reports of that day was the fact that Arsenal needed to win to qualify for the UEFA Cup so they were really up for it.

Entering the ground from the left side (of course) of the Clock End we bumped into Pelé (as you do) who for some strange reason was there that day. Why he was walking from the Clock End to the stand I have no idea. The atmosphere had been pretty lively but turned moody before kick off when loads of Arsenal fans came charging down the stand on the left looking for trouble. I actually felt for the kids who got stuck in to them and subsequently arrested, as they doubtless missed the most important Villa game in years, as well as probably having to spend the night in the cells and copping a thumping fine too.

The game itself was hell on earth – the Villa seemed to freeze and play with lead in their boots and the two goals seemed to be conceded in slow motion. We were truly awful. At half-time we were in the pits of despair and I felt as physically sick as I ever have done in my life with the Villa.

We all know that Bosko saved the day – just as well as we were never, ever going to trouble Arsenal ourselves. The rumours from blokes with radios did start to change the mood but I was convinced that Ipswich would come back from the dead and that all the radio rumours were incorrect. That famous clock behind us went a round as slowly as any other in history, a record it was to hold until another clock in Rotterdam seemed to be broken for 26 minutes a year later.

The final whistle was as much relief as ecstasy. Within seconds thousands of Arsenal fans were on the pitch from the North Bank and the police managed to form a cordon. The atmosphere was very ugly as I reckon they were determined not to let us celebrate on their pitch, and without the police it would have been really nasty as Villa obviously had a fair number of nutters out that day. We got onto the pitch ourselves and picked up some turf, but it all felt surreal – celebrating the title after our worst performance of the season.

We decided to head to Victoria to get a National Express back to Brum as none of us wanted to get home at three in the morning. Getting back to the tube was a battle as the police stopped us going to Arsenal and pointed us to Finsbury Park where loads of 'Gooners' were looking for Villa fans. The police told us to shut our traps and we would be fine but there were only five of us and it got a bit hairy. Some kids from our estate were in the tube carriage next to ours and the Arsenal fans wandering around got in with them and one of the Pheasey lads was stabbed. We found out the next day he needed stitches but it was not too serious. We managed to get a coach back to Brum. One of my mates leant me the fare and I got back in time for one pint (thanks to my mates again) in the Pen and Wig in Dale End before 10.30 closing and the last bus home. We were so mentally and physically exhausted that none of us could get up next morning to see the trophy being presented at the Town Hall.

It truly was a strange way to win the League (and one hell of a day out) and I have always rued the lack of sheer elation and absolute adrenaline that should have come from our last title win. Satisfaction yes, but not 100 per cent unrestrained joy. On the coach home we were talking as much about getting to Wembley as having won the League – none of us had gone to Wembley in 1977 due to family unemployment. We knew it was a great achievement but in comparison I have felt more elation after Final wins. Not to worry: the unadulterated joy of Rotterdam a year later was the consummate example of what winning a trophy really felt like. Surely the future would always be like this we all thought?
Pat McMahon, Shanghai, China.

My own memories as a 16-year-old on the day consist mainly of attempting to secure booze from any 'offy' that would sell us some and trying to act hard outside Highbury. Then it was 'Hell on the Clock End' as we gathered around anyone with a transistor radio as rumours of Bosco's heroics filtered through.

I seem to remember Peter Withe coming over at one point during the game to ask us what was happening as we were all celebrating Boro's second goal; it must have been surreal being a player on the pitch being stuffed by Arsenal but potentially still winning the League. The end of the match was a blur, I was near the front so had no choice but to go onto the pitch; I was just swept along, me and my mate just sheltered in the goalmouth punching each other and yelling 'Yeeessssssssss!!' continuously. Never did get our bus back to Birmingham. Luckily my mate had a rich(ish) dad so he stumped up the train fares instead.

Dave Cooper, Biarritz, France.

I will always recall the last game of the 1980–81 season at Highbury and the vast amount of support we had that day. Villa took the whole of the Clock End and probably filled half of the ground in all. Even though we lost the game it was still a good day. I don't remember the game as I was more interested in listening to reports on the Ipswich game on the radio. There was a 'funny' atmosphere when we left Highbury as we had lost the game but won the League.

Steve Eccles, Lichfield, Staffordshire.

Turf Moor   26 August 1972
Burnley 4 Villa 1

It was our second away game of the season. As the 'Special' pulled out of Burnley station, we got bricked by some kids at the top of the cutting. My mate was hurling abuse at them, only to get hit straight between the eyes on the bridge of his nose with a rock. I've never seen so much blood in my life! He's still got the scar to this day.

Ken Baldwin, Lichfield, Staffordshire.

Turf Moor   26 February 1974, FA Cup fifth round
Burnley 1 Villa 0

I travelled from Croydon to Burnley for that game – a long trip. We fought hard against a team who were in the top flight at the time but we just weren't good enough. That was really the story of our season, apart from the heroics against Arsenal the previous round. Vic Crowe and Ron Wylie were sacked at the end of the season, when it became obvious that they could take the club no further. They were replaced by Ron Saunders, and the glory years were about to begin.

Frank, Horsham, West Sussex.

Eastville   2 October 1971
Bristol Rovers 0 Villa 1

This would probably have been the 1971–72 season when Villa were promoted from Division Three. My uncle took me to Bristol and I remember standing at the front of the stand, near the centre line. Villa won as I recall. The match sticks in my memory though, because of the hooligans. Leaving the ground things got quite hairy and I can remember walking along a road with a wall of Rovers fans coming towards us. My uncle made me hide my Villa scarf and we dodged into a shop until they'd passed.
Kevin Pitt, Walsall, West Midlands.

Belle View   29 November 2005, League Cup fourth round
Doncaster Rovers 3 Villa 0

I was in the car park after watching the players get back on the coach. Then Mr O'Leary came out and was signing autographs for a few 'Donny' fans still there. In a completely non-confrontational manner I calmly said to him 'Excuse me Mr O'Leary, could you please give me any reason why I have just watched the worst display by an Aston Villa team in 40 years?' He looked up at me, paused for a moment, then turned round and walked off! Thanks for the memory, Mr O'Leary!!
Roger Hatfield, Sutton Coldfield, West Midlands.

Valley Parade   6 February 1971
Bradford City 1 Villa 0

I remember travelling to Bradford City for a Third Division game in February 1971 and as usual in those days you looked out for the floodlights and headed in that general direction. However, we ended up at Park Avenue home to Bradford Park Avenue, a somewhat dilapidated but what once was an impressive ground from Edwardian times. I can still remember the Dolls House in the corner. Bradford PA had lost their place in the League a couple of years before and were then in the Northern League but were away; however it took us sometime to escape as the car park man insisted we forget the Villa match and watch their Reserves against Fleetwood Town Reserves. Perhaps we should have stayed as Villa lost 1–0 to Bradford City at Valley Parade and I always wondered how their Reserves faired. Nice to see Bradford PA making a comeback in the Evo-Stick Premier League but not at their Park Avenue ground.

Other trips include going to Bury in my old Mini and following a car with claret and blue scarves out of the window and ending up at Burnden Park for Bolton v West Ham! Which reminds me of a time when going to Bolton's old ground in the 1970s with my Mum, Dad and my brother and getting lost after the game. After what seemed ages driving around we stopped at some traffic lights and Dad, who by this time had turned the air blue, shouted at the bloke in the car alongside, 'what's the name of this b****y town' and the reply came back in that fabulous Bolton accent, 'It's Bolton lad'. I've never seen anyone change their mood so fast as my Dad and we all ended up in fits of laughter.

I remember another trip to Millmoor, Rotherham around 1972 with my ex-wife. We had just joined the M6 north (yep that's right) at Great Barr when some coaches full of Manchester United fans heading to a home match were on the inside lane. So I told my ex-wife to put my claret and blue scarf out of the window to show the colours. So what did she do? She threw it out instead of trapping it in the window! Then when I saw the turn for Stafford I realised I should have been heading to Yorkshire instead of Lancashire, so a quick detour east and just made it in time but all in vain as we lost 2–1.

John Hatfield, Sutton Coldfield, West Midlands.

Stadium of Light   15 December 2007
Sunderland 1 Villa 1

We got lost going to Sunderland for the 1–1 draw a couple of seasons ago. My mate's old man was driving, we printed the directions off the internet and were following them but they were directing us the wrong way so we stopped at a service station and asked an RAC bloke for directions. It turned out his directions were completely wrong as well and we ended up in Carlisle (nowhere near Sunderland). We had to go in the tourist centre, buy an A-Z and ask the old woman in there to draw a line in it to Sunderland from where we were, and her directions got us there eventually. We left the house at 9am and got in the ground at 2.30pm, and to top it all off I had the worst, flattest pint of beer when I got in the ground. Five and a half hours in a car gasping for a pint and I got served what looked like a pint of dish water. Oh and the weather was freezing too!

Steven Brown, Black Country.

Sellhurst Park   11 September 1973
Crystal Palace 0 Villa 0

We went to Crystal Palace in the early 1970s. A guy in the car we were travelling with said he knew exactly where to go and was directing the

driver. We did have a map but got a bit confused by the route. After a while he says triumphantly, 'stop the car and you can put that map away now, we're there'. We were there all right!! At Craven Cottage!
John P. Knibb, Birmingham.

Plough Lane   25 November 1989.

Wimbledon 0 Villa 2

I'll never forget going to Wimbledon in November 1989. The first and only time I ever went there (thank God!). The four of us got to London at around midday. All we had to do was drive through London and get to the ground. Even for London standards, the traffic was horrendous and it took hours but we eventually got south of the river and were running out of time and started to panic, looking through the A-Z for clues. We were totally lost but eventually reached the ground 30 minutes after the kick off!! At least we got in but missed David Platt putting us 1–0 up. We eventually won 2–0 with a crowd of less than 6,000, with about half of them being Villa fans.
Charlie Smith, Kidderminster, Worcestershire.

Craven Cottage   18 September 1965

Fulham 3 Villa 6

In September 1965 we headed off to our favourite London ground, Craven Cottage with not a lot of hope. From the high hopes of 'Mercer's Minors' we were now in our second decline and fall. Amazingly, we won the game 6–3 and we made our way to the tube station and a night in the 'Smoke'. Who did we bump into on the station? None other than Villa skipper Phil Woosenam, who was off to stay with relatives. 'Great game Phil,' we said and he replied 'Yes, I've just phoned my report through to the Argus and at first they did not believe me'. We all laughed and we wished him well. We lost the return game at Villa Park 5–2, and although we survived relegation it was only to put off the inevitable.
Robert Dore, Birmingham.

Heroes and Villains

This section is a compilation of events, players habits and snipits of games which stuck out in people's memories. They are all randomly chosen so enjoy and recap some good and bad memories and remember the heroes and villains of the past.

- Paul McGrath – remember those flying back heels?

- Olof Melburg – 'I've just got the feeling that I just don't like Birmingham City at all.'

- Mark Bosnich – when the ball was up the other end you'd see him stretching his arms out to the side and to the sky like Mad Lizzie from TVam.

- Gordon Cowans – His pose when he took a free-kick – one leg trailing behind and pointing down to the floor and his 'turn' – where he'd drag the ball round behind him changing feet and beating his marker. Pure brilliance!

- Dean Saunders – running with his tongue out all the time.

- Shaun Teale – making a fantastic challenge then hobbling about for the next two minutes.

- Peter Withe – and his bag of sweets from the lady in the Witton Lane stand and his famous claret and blue sweat bands.

- Brian Little – never having his shirt tucked in and socks always round his ankles.

- Juan Pablo Angel's headband.

- John Gregory and his lollipop.

- Savo's bandana.

- Dwight Yorke – running up the length of the pitch towards the tunnel after every pre-match warm up with the ball balanced on his head. Amazing!

- Ashley Young – looking like he was about to cry whenever he was awarded a free-kick.

- Dalian Atkinson – sleeping on the halfway line.

- Spinksy's tongue in his chin when he was concentrating!

- The claret and blue Mini Metro that used to drive around the perimeter of the pitch at half-time.

- Jimmy Rimmer – illegally 'marking' his six-yard area before the start of each half.

- ⚽ Alpay – receiving a hero's reception at the end of each game, bowing to all four corners of Villa Park.

- ⚽ Ashley Young's hands on both knees, wincing in pain then hobbling around after he has been fouled.

- ⚽ Tony Daley – with a bit of space belting it up the Trinity Road by-line and the whole of the stand jumping out of their seats.

- ⚽ Dwight Yorke's chipped pen at Sheffield United. Everyone stood there and thinking has he really done that?

- ⚽ Dalian Atkinson's wagging his fingers when he scored as he ran off towards the corner flag.

- ⚽ Gary Shaw's non-celebration of goals.

- ⚽ Ugo's loping giraffe-like stride.

- ⚽ The 'AV' floodlights (a la 1970s).

- ⚽ Stevie Staunton's out swingers into the Trinity Road stand (and his goal direct from a corner).

- ⚽ Tony Morley's gestures to Ron Saunders after scoring. Flicking the 'Vs'.

- ⚽ The lettered scoreboard (a la 1970s).

- ⚽ The Trinity Road clock - RIP!.

- ⚽ The dummy/step over McGrath, and then Ugo, used to always do when ball was heading for a goal kick.

- ⚽ 'Bozzie' tapping the top of the cross bar before a corner was taken.

- ⚽ Peter Enckleman v Birmingham City – say no more!

- ⚽ Thomas Sorensen v Birminghm City – Don't even go there!

- ⚽ Garry Parker v Norwich – missed a sitter.

- ⚽ Juan Pablo Angel v Tottenham – own-goal, missed penalty and kicked the flag onto ball trying to take a quick corner causing it to go out for a goal kick.

- ⚽ Derek Mountfield v Norwich – own-goals (twice).

- ⚽ Bosko Balaban – £6 million? He only started 11 games and failed to score.

- ⚽ Savo – bought on the evidence of a video.

- ⚽ Doncaster 3 Villa 0 – Sends shudders down your spine thinking about it, Mr O'Leary.

- ⚽ Steve Hodge's backpass - not good.

- ⚽ Mark Bosnich's Nazi salute at White Hart Lane. Shameful!

- Chelsea 7–1. What can be said about that? And we finished 6th in the League!

- Oxford City away in the League Cup semi-final.

- Losing 5–0 against Notts Forest in the 1980s with Trevor Christie taking us apart. Trevor who?

- Losing 4–1 to Coventry City at home in the FA Cup.

- Savo spitting at Blackburn. Disgraceful!

- Losing at home to Oldham to end the dream.

- Losing a 4–1 lead at Tottenham only to draw 4–4. But what a game!

- Dion Dublin giving Robby Savage a 'Glasgow kiss'.

- Losing 5–0 v Bradford in front of 4,000.

- Chris Nicholl scoring all four goals in a 2–2 draw against Leicester City.

- 4–1 up at home to Leicester City with 10 minutes to go and drawing 4–4.

- Ugo's debut. Say no more!

- Defending League champions in 1982 starting their defence of the title with a 1–0 home defeat to newly promoted Notts County. (We regularly lost to Notts County, even though they were rubbish).

- The 'Champions of Europe' being beaten on the opening day of the season 3–1 by Sunderland of all teams, followed a few days later with a 5–0 thrashing at Everton. Surely the worst two results by any club in it's first two competitive games after winning the European Cup?

- The 6–0 defeat in 1986 when we waved to Cloughie and he waved back? And we started celebrating their goals? He was a genius it has to be said!

- Stan Collymore's home debut against Blackburn. It was 0–3 at half-time and finished 0–4.

- Losing 7–1 to Arsenal at Villa Park, 14 December, 1935. Who remembers that?

- Losing 5–1 at home to Man City in 1991 – that's when they were rubbish!

- FA Cup Final 2000. Case closed!! Worse Cup Final ever?

- Forest 6–0, Southampton 5–0 and Charlton 3–0 under Billy McNeill. Lost!

- Losing 3–0 at Oldham in the FA Cup.

- 03.03.03 – losing at home to our 'dear' neighbours from Small Heath after they beat us at St Andrews 3–0 in the September. Awful in every way imaginable and how embarrassing!!

- The abject surrender of a 2–0 lead to Hull City only to lose 3–2 in the last few minutes on a grey, grey afternoon in November 1967 made me realise we really were rubbish and getting back to the First Division was not going to be happening any time soon.

- ⚽ Rioting at Anderlecht. - shocking!

- ⚽ The Glasgow Rangers 'friendly'. - Never again!

- ⚽ Trying to offload Brian Little to Blues.

- ⚽ Ron Saunders joining Blues – how could you Ron?

- ⚽ Demolishing the Trinity Road stand.

- ⚽ 2–0 up against Man United with 15 minutes to go and they brought Roy Keane and Van Nistelrooy off the bench.

- ⚽ A home defeat by Coventry City in the Cup in the late 1990s. Up until then we'd always sing 'You'll never beat the Villa' to them. Then they beat the Villa.

- ⚽ Losing 6–1 v Arsenal in 1983.

- ⚽ Losing 5–0 at Leicester in 1984 which was a 11am kick off for some strange reason – unusual in those days.

- ⚽ Leeds in April 1995. Carlton Palmer got the only goal of the game at Elland Road and I think it was in the last few minutes. I remember seeing the little piece about it on *Final Score* and the voice-over ended with something like 'It'll be a miracle if Villa survive' or similar. I really, really thought we were down that day and I went up to my room and cried for about 20 minutes.

- ⚽ Going down to the old Third Division in the early 1970s. Dark days indeed.

- ⚽ Losing on the opening day of the 1979–80 season to newly promoted Bristol City.

- ⚽ Losing at home to Second Division Fulham in the FA Cup in 1998–99. I really did think we were going to win the League that season.

- ⚽ Villa 0 Southampton 0 on a freezing cold day and only 8,000 people at Villa Park. A very, very sad sight indeed.

- ⚽ At home to Spartak Moscow in the UEFA Cup in November 1983. Thought we were on the up. Mark Walters was the second coming of Cruyff and the UEFA Cup was in the bag.

- ⚽ Villa 0 Southampton 2, It snowed all game, nobody could stand up except for Matt 'I Hate Villa' Le Tissier who scored two.

- ⚽ Losing 1–0 at home to Sheffield Wednesday – when Les Sealey (God rest him) dived the ball over the line from Nigel Jemson. George Courtney gave the goal despite being chased all round the pitch by 'Says Les'.

- ⚽ Oldham at home the week before the 1994 League Cup Final. Eleven disinterested Villa players handing the points to a relegation-battling

Oldham side. Our only goal came when one of their players needlessly tucked a Steve Froggatt cross into his own net. Big Ron said after the game, 'You heard the booing? I started it.'

❉ Nothing to do with the team, but the infamous skydiving accident at half-time of the Arsenal game in 1998 was a terrible thing to see. I can still hear the thud ringing around Villa Park. He was the last one to come in and it was apparent to my novice skydiving eye that he was not going to make it. On the plus side though was the fact that the half-time got delayed and we came back to win.

❉ Losing 6–0 at Newcastle and embarrassed by Rapid Vienna twice in a year!!

❉ The 3–0 defeat on Oldham's plastic pitch in the 1990 FA Cup semi-final.

❉ Vicarage Road, Watford on 13 September 1969. Watford were awful and they beat us 3–0. That's how bad we were. Some poor lad whose name escapes me made his debut at full back and was never seen again.

❉ Losing to Wimbledon at Villa Park in the FA Cup around 1989–90 with the goal line scrambled goal they scored. Even at the time of watching it, the ball seemed to trickle into the Holte End net in slow motion. It was the Saturday after we beat 'Spurs 2–0 and if we won, we would've gone five points clear of Liverpool. David Platt missed a penalty at 0–0, then they took us apart. Our season started to fall apart from then on.

❉ Blues (rock bottom of the League) 3 Villa (European champions) 0 Boxing Day 1982 – how can that be?

❉ Season 1986–87 – bottom of the League! Does it get any worse?

❉ Villa 0 Coventry 0 in 1993. Walking out of the ground and finding out Manchester United were still playing time added on against Sheffield Wednesday – 10 minutes of it!!!

❉ Getting beat by Tranmere away in the League Cup Semi-Final, even though Dalian Atkinson got one back to give us hope. I remember the journey back to Birmingham on the coach. It was silent so the driver starts playing Beatles songs to wind us up!!!

❉ The FA Cup quarter-final away at Oldham 1989–90. Bernie Gallagher on the wing, our fans fighting each other, Rick Holden playing like Johan Cruyff – a terrible nightmare!!!

❉ Graham Turner's last game in the 6–0 defeat at Forest. Just when we thought it couldn't get any worse!!

❉ The (short) reign of Billy McNeill – oh, it did get worse!

❉ The Steve Hodge back pass against Norwich City in 1987. Probably the most memorable moment of that season.

- Doncaster Rovers in the League Cup in 2005. Even more embarrassing it was live on Sky.

- Losing 3–0 at home to Spurs in the first game of the 1986–87 season. So optimistic, we were tipped to do well by some that season. After 30 minutes we knew we were in deep, deep trouble for the rest of the season.

- The 3–0 away defeat at Coventry in 1989–90. Mickey Quinn hat trick and it kicked off everywhere and how they loved it too. It was their Cup Final.

- Being robbed by Stern John in the third minute of injury time at home against Blues in 2002.

- The Dean Saunders's goal against Ipswich at Villa Park. - Cracking!

- Chris Nicholl's belter at Old Trafford against Everton in the LC Final.

- Paul Merson's goal at Goodison Park 2000.

- Stilyian Petrov's 50-yarder at Derby.

- Benito Carbone in the Cup against Leeds.

- Savo's stunner in the League Cup Final at Wembley.

- Brian Little's run in the 1977 Old Trafford second replay final.

- Andy Lochhead's header in the 1970–71 semi-final at Villa Park against Manchester United.

- Practically all of Lee Hendrie's goals were 'pearlers', even his most hardened critics would have to agree.

- Andy Townsend's goal at Chelsea – 1996–97.

- Tony Morley's run from the edge of his box in East Germany in our European Cup run and his goal at Everton in the same season.

- Brian Little's overhead kick goal v Manchester City in League Cup 1976–77.

- 19 August 1995, Villa Park, scorching sunshine. Manchester United are the visitors and they are already 1–0 down. Alan Wright disposes of Phil Neville with an excellent slide tackle and then slips the ball to Mark Draper. Draper touches it on to Yorke who sets off on a long run up to the edge of the penalty box. He gives it to Milosevic who nutmegs a challenge and passes it to Draper who has made the run from deep inside his own half. Terrific placed shot, 2–0 Villa. One of the best Villa moves ever.

- And finally who could forget...
  "Shaw, Williams, prepared to venture down the left. There's a good ball. Played in for Tony Morley. Oh, it must be! And it is! Peter Withe. Villa in the lead!"

Far, Far Away

I t is a proven scientific fact that the most important goal in the history of English football was scored by Peter Withe in the Feyenoord Stadium in the 68th minute of the European Cup Final on 26 May 1982. Typically, cynics have tended to concentrate on the scruffy nature of Withe's finish, the ball rebounding off his shin and into the Bayern Munich net for the only goal of the game. But, as the Villa number nine has pointed out many times, if he had made clean contact, Manfred Muller, the Bayern Munich goalkeeper, may well have been able to make a save. And focusing on the final act obscures the sheer beauty of the build-up, in the words of the late Brian Moore:

'Shaw. Williams, prepared to venture down the left. There's a good ball played in for Tony Morley,' [who crosses it to Peter Withe]. Oh, it must be! And it is! Peter Withe. Villa in the lead.'

This section is dedicated to those European nights which are so special to both players and fans alike because they are 'one offs' and a diversification from the pressures of domestic football.

☉

Gordon 'Sid' Cowans started his career as a Villa apprentice in 1974, and signed as a professional for the club in 1976. During his time at Aston Villa, he won the League Cup, the League Championship, the European Cup and the European Super Cup. He left Villa for the first time in 1985, signing for Italian club, Bari. He then returned in 1988 and left again in 1991 moving to Blackburn Rovers. When he left Blackburn he came back to Villa, before moving to Derby County, Wolverhampton Wanderers, Sheffield United, Bradford City, Stockport County and finally Burnley. Capped 10 times for England, Gordon is now first team coach under Alex McLeish.

I've got some great memories of playing for Villa but the abiding memory has to be the 1982 European Cup Final. Against all odds we weren't given a chance. However, although we were the underdogs we knew we had a chance because our team spirit and togetherness was unbelievable. Obviously, we had some good players as well.

On the day, I don't think anyone was over-awed; we all took it in our stride. It was strange really. We went out onto the pitch before the game and took pictures of each other and we were pretty relaxed really. The build up obviously helped. Tony Barton, the way he was, he was a pretty relaxed man so we went out there and gave it everything. Thankfully, we got the rewards.

Strangely, it took a while for it to sink in that we had actually won the European Cup. Obviously, it's the biggest achievement in your career to win the European Cup, but it was doubly difficult at the time because you had to win the League to actually qualify for the competition; now you only have to finish in the top four. To actually win the League was difficult in itself back then, with Liverpool winning it several times in a row it was a fantastic achievement for us.

Gordon Cowans, former Villa midfielder, 1976–85, 1988–91 and 1993–94.

Gary Shaw was the golden boy of the Villa side in the early 1980s. His 18 goals helped Villa win the Division One Championship in 1980–81 and the European Cup the following year and he was the only Birmingham-born player in the team. In 1981 he was voted PFA Young Player of the Year and a year later he was voted European Young Player of the Year. Gary talks about his European adventures in Japan and the Toyota Cup against C.A. Peñarol of Uruguay and in the European Super Cup against FC Barcelona at a time when Villa were on top of the world.

We played Arsenal at Highbury on the Tuesday night and then flew out to Tokyo on the Wednesday. We didn't arrive there until Thursday and the game was on Sunday, so we only had two days acclimatisation after travelling halfway around the world.

It was a full house and there was very big interest in the game. A few Villa fans that could afford to make the trip went over to Japan, but the stadium was primarily full of locals. It was a strange atmosphere and unlike anything I had experienced ever before. There was a constant buzz around the terraces and it seemed to get a little bit higher whenever there were any signs of goalmouth action. Whenever we went out for a walk around the city prior to the game there were always lots of Japanese schoolgirls following us round, which was bizarre. They were only in the formative years of their League in those days, so we were considered big stars.

We played against Peñarol and did pretty well in the first half and we were the better team. We hit the bar and some half chances, so felt reasonably confident even though it was goalless. They scored against the

run of play from a free-kick after the break and then got another goal late on when we were chasing the game. Considering it was being billed as a match between the best two club teams in the world we weren't given a lot of preparation time. I am not sure how the Uruguayans prepared, but it was squeezed in between our League fixtures.

It is a different format now but the exposure was totally different. All we got was two minutes

Gary Shaw playing for Villa 1982–83 season.

on a sports bulletin on local television! I think there was live coverage on local radio, but that was about it really.

We also played against Barcelona in the European Super Cup later on that season and in those days it took place over two legs on a home and away basis. Diego Maradona was playing for them at that time but fortunately for us he was injured so he did not play in either fixture. They still had people of the calibre of Berndt Schuster playing for them, so it was always going to be a tough game.

The first leg was in the Nou Camp and I think that while there was a crowd of over 45,000 it didn't seem like that many in a stadium that holds over 100,000. We lost 1–0 in Spain but we beat them 3–0 at Villa Park after extra-time a week later to lift the trophy. We had Allan Evans sent off and they had two players sent off and that probably cost us in our European Cup campaign. He was suspended for the quarter-final against Juventus and I think it might have been a different result if we had Allan playing at the back as he was such an influential player for us.

Gary Shaw, former Villa forward, 1978–88.

Ken McNaught played for Aston Villa and was part of the Championship winning side of 1981, the European Cup side in 1982 and also won the European Super Cup in 1983 against Barcelona, scoring one of Villa's goals in the latter Final.

My outstanding memory of playing for Villa is the European Super Cup in 1983 against Barcelona. Denis (Mortimer) was injured and I was captain for the second leg at Villa Park. We were 1–0 down after the First Leg over in Barcelona. We managed to scrape it back to equalise and then won it in extra-time. I managed to score as well and it made it one of those 'special' European evenings you get at Villa Park.

There weren't too many superstars in their side at the time but they were still 'Barcelona'. They had won the European Cup Winners Cup in 1982 and had a decent side. The only player that stood out for me was their big centre-half, Miguel Bernardo Bianquetti (aka Migueli) who was captain of Spain at the time. He was a top performer for Barcelona for many years.

Another Memorable European game was my first for Villa against Polish side Górnik Zabrze in the 2nd Round of the 1977 UEFA Cup at Villa Park. I had signed for Villa at the end of the 1976–77 season and didn't settle in too quickly but we won 2–0 and I scored both goals that night and from then on, it all came good for me.

I formed a good partnership with Allan Evans, who came down from Dunfermline as a striker originally around the same time as me; I think he was the most expensive teenager to come out of Scotland at the time. I watched him play up front but had a word with Ron Saunders and recommended he played at the back because he was big built and had a bit of pace. Ron listened and from then on played him at centre-back alongside myself. Ron changed a lot in the time I knew him; when I first went to Villa he was a 'Sergeant Major' type but then the better the players he brought in, he would trust them more and he started to ask players questions. Every time he asked me about players I'd always give him an honest answer; I told Ron that Allan wouldn't make it as a striker in England so he gave him a try-out in training and we quickly developed a great understanding as centre-half partners.

Ken McNaught, former Villa centre-back, 1977–83.

Pat Heard moved to Aston Villa in 1979 but failed to hold down a regular spot but nonetheless gained a European Cup medal after being named as a non-playing substitute for the 1982 European Cup Final. Pat now co-commentates on Villa's games on BRMB Radio.

Although I was not part of the League Championship team I was part of the European Cup squad of 1982. I actually had a heart complaint when I was with Villa at the age of 21 and it forced me out of the team during the Championship year but I managed to get back into the reckoning just before the 1982 European Cup Final.

I remember going to the Final. It was basically treated as a 'normal' game. I can't really remember it being hyped up too much, like games these days are, what with Sky TV and all the coverage big matches get.

Tony Morley, Gordon Cowans and Pat Heard holding the European Cup in Rotterdam, 1982.

When we turned up at the ground, we had our blazers, shirts and ties on looking smart. I can remember coming out of the tunnel and seeing all these German guys walking past us in flip-flops and shorts. I was thinking, 'Was that Paul Brighner? Was that Karl-Heinz Rummenigge? Hang on a minute, are they taking this game seriously?' We honestly thought they had never heard of Aston Villa FC they were that cool about the game.

Just being on the bench and watching the lads was a tremendous honour. Then after the game we were in the players' lounge and I remember Tony Morley had been pulled to one side to take a random drugs test and I was sitting there drinking beer and having a chat then we had an hour's coach journey from Rotterdam back to Amsterdam where there was a function in the evening. By the time we got back to Amsterdam, most of the players had had enough to drink. The trophy had been passed around a lot on the coach, everyone had their photos taken with it. What I remember most of that journey was the European Cup trophy was eventually put in the bowl of the toilet of the coach. So, if anyone wanted to use the toilet, you'd have to pull the Cup out of the bowl first.

I would have loved to have got onto the pitch but that team named itself and everyone can name the starting line-up; it was the same team, week in, week out. The only player to have dropped out of that team was Eamon Deacy. The only time when the team changed was when Ron Saunders resigned and Tony Barton took over. Leading up to the Final, I remember playing down at Highbury and Denis Mortimer was rested, which was very rare in those days and I was playing at left midfield and Tony (Morley) was pushed out to right midfield. We got beat 4–3 that day but I happened to score a goal and Tony actually scored with a rare header.

The squad had a good mix, with the older generation and the likes of Denis Mortimer, and we had the younger generation with the likes of Gordon Cowans, myself, Tony Morley and Gary Shaw. Everyone got on really well. Nobody ever fell out with anybody else and I mean that. It was just a dream team. Nobody was 'bigger' than anybody else, nobody talked behind anybody's back. It obviously helped us be successful. Every Tuesday or Wednesday afternoon, there would be 10 or 12 of us down at The Belfry Hotel having a drink. Honestly, you didn't feel walking out of the dressing room that anyone would say anything about you. It never happened. We were all in it together. We didn't know who earned what money (well I didn't, anyway as I was only 21 at the time). It was such a good dressing room.

Even though I didn't get on the pitch, I will be remembered in Aston Villa history as being part of that squad and I am very modest about it and proud to be associated with that squad. I wouldn't change anything and I'm so glad it happened because I had a heart complaint and I didn't get back into the squad until after Christmas (of 1981) so every time the European Cup win comes up, my name is mentioned.

A genuine 1982 European Cup Final ticket.

However, one of the games that many people will remember was a game against West Bromwich Albion at The Hawthorns (8 March 1982). We had a free-kick awarded in the last minute of the game. Denis (Mortimer) tapped it to one side and, basically, I hit it and it flew into the back of the net to win us the game.
Pat Heard, former Villa midfielder, 1979–83.

In the run up to the 1982 European Cup Final I won a caption competition in the *Evening Mail* and for which the prize was an all expenses paid trip to the game for myself and a mate. It was a great trip, an even better result and something that I will remember forever. I will also never forget that one of the guys on the trip missed the coach from the out of town hotel to the ground and somehow missed the greatest experience to date for any Villa supporter.
Paul Farrington, Halesowen, West Midlands.

I'm a 53-year-old Villa fan, exiled to Yorkshire through work. As a teenager I used to follow the claret and blue home and away and I still see the occasional game. One of my many memories was the morning after our fantastic European Cup victory in Rotterdam.

To get there, we had travelled by special train, ferry and coach. We had celebrated our victory only briefly because we had to get the coach back to Boulogne. We arrived there at around 4.00 am, with the ferry home due to set sail at about 6.30 am. We all sat around, several hundred fans, mainly on the floor, in a fairly bleak ferry terminal where nothing was open. Spirits were still high after the win but tiredness and fatigue was creeping in.

Then two Villa fans stood up and started singing *The Music Man*. Well these two guys really went through their full repertoire ... trumpet, drums, piano, banjo and so on and so on. Then one of them sang, 'I am the music man, they tell me I can sing ... what do you sing ... I can sing ... There's only one Aston Villa' ... to which everyone stood up and launched into song. It was just so spontaneous, uplifting, funny and truly memorable.
Gary Horton, Bingley, West Yorkshire.

In 1975, as staunch Villa supporters, my mate Phil and I were planning a trip to see Villa play away against Royal Antwerp in the UEFA Cup in their first ever European game. Another mate, who had no interest in football was persuaded to come with us. We all went, as part of a small band of Villa supporters, on a trip organised by Ellis Travel. It was a long and tiring journey which included a third class return train journey in Belgium, which

in itself has to be somewhat unique. In the end we lost 4–1, although we all otherwise had a great time. Now 36 years later, that football match still remains the only game that our friend has ever attended.
Paul Farrington, Halesowen, West Midlands.

I was only young at the time but I went to the 1982 European Cup semi-final in Belgium against Anderlecht and to the Final in Rotterdam. I travelled by coach from Burntwood with some friends to Rotterdam – I'll never forget all the coaches parked up. I saw many people sleeping overnight in the hedgerows and fans worse for wear because of the drink. The city was divided into two; the Bayern Munich fans in one half and the Villa fans in the other. There was no trouble whatsoever (as far as I can remember). I was a bit overawed at the final. It was a great atmosphere inside the stadium. I didn't really take it all in. I remember we didn't play too well during the 90 minutes; Bayern Munich played well but we won it on the day and that's all that mattered. It was still awesome all the same.
Steve Eccles, Lichfield, Staffordshire.

Leaving Rotterdam aside, my favourite places were Royal Antwerp in 1975, even though it was as good as over by half-time (was it 4–0 at half-time) it was still our very first foray on foreign soil and a big sign that we were returning. Then in 1977 going to Atletico Bilbao. I sat behind the goal and we were amongst Spanish fans who kept passing round what seemed an endless supply of red wine. They were a great bunch even though they managed to relieve me of my Union Jack flag when I staggering round the streets in the early hours. I shouldn't complain really as I'd nicked it in the first place a week earlier from the flagpole off the Conservative club after another drinking session.
Paul Smith, Birmingham.

I've been to 10 European away games and have loads of memories, hardly any bad ones either. One that sticks in the mind was Gornik Zabrze in 1977–78, mainly because there were only about 40 of us that went. It was before the Iron Curtain came down. We flew into Warsaw, and then faced a five hour coach trip to the Holiday Inn, Krakow, before another hour's trip to Zabrze itself. Poland certainly lived up to the stereotypical Eastern European country, grim weather, no leaves on the trees, military types with machine guns watching our every move, drab, austere buildings and no fast food joints!

The game finished 1–1 and we returned to the hotel after the game. We were in the restaurant, when the door opened and in came the full Villa party. Their charter flight had been postponed until the next day due to the heavy fog and they were stopping the night at our hotel. I got some nice photos of myself with Andy Gray, Frank Carrodus and Alex Cropley

Villa fans travelling to Gornik in November 1977.

amongst others. Deadly Doug came round every single fan in the room and shook their hand and thanked us for travelling to support the boys. The only downside was when I had to share the lift later on with Gary Newbon, who was with Central at the time!

Terry Weir took a group photo of us next morning, which appeared in a subsequent Villa programme.

It was nearly 33 years ago, but I can remember it like yesterday. As I can remember a group of us being mistaken for Villa players in a restaurant on the banks of the Bosphorus before the Fenerbache game in September 1977, but that's another story...

Ken Baldwin, Lichfield, Staffordshire.

There have been many great trips; each with their own tales. I remember the visit to Berlin which was made even better by the fact that it was played behind the Berlin Wall. We arrived there about nine in the morning, by train, and after all the performance of getting through the security and collecting our ration of East German Marks, we set off for a pub (where else?). There was a bar near the ground that served the purpose and we sat in there all day until about half an hour before the game. The beer was the equivalent of 25p per pint and we must have had two gallons each. For food we had kartoffel suppe mit bratwurst. It came in a white plastic bowl and was thin potato soup with a sausage dumped in it. Lovely!

The game was memorable for Tony Morley's goals. There was a bit of trouble immediately after the game but we had to get to the station for midnight as our Visa would run out and we would miss the train. Following all the beer, I felt extremely rough but this changed when the attendant came to the carriage and asked if we would like tea. It was served in a plastic tea pot, one each, and did the trick instantly.

However, the tram we were travelling on became derailed in Antwerp and that was another story. Villa ran a 'special' to that match. Two Black Country blokes who came to Bucharest chanced on the same bar as us and proclaimed, to their delight, 'we'm struck 'ere mar mate, ay we?' I found them later that night on a balcony in a lift lobby. They were trapped there and couldn't get back into the hotel. A familiar cry came from them, 'we'm stuck mate!'

Recent trips have concentrated on having the best food and drink that is on offer and it is things like that which make you return for more.
Jon P. Knibb, Birmingham.

Inter Milan in 1990. We stayed in France on the Tuesday night and six of us got hammered with the locals in a little bar. When we left the bar was decorated with Villa scarves and we all had St Etienne souvenirs, the only thing I've got to show I went to the San Siro and not St Etienne is my ticket stub. Back on the coach the next morning one of the lads had handcuffs hanging from one wrist as a legacy of the night before! Can't remember how or if he got them off before the game.
Tony Roberts, Birmingham.

Bucharest 1997. We travelled with Goughy's Coaches. There was only about 30 of us and it took us a week to get there and back. We stopped off in Vienna a couple of nights too. The match was rubbish, we lost 2–1 I think but the trip was a real eye opener. Bucharest was a typical eastern European city; dark and grim. I remember our hotel running out of milk at breakfast, and drinking in a pub in the centre called The George! I also remember after the match, when we got back on the coach, the British Ambassador in Bucharest got on the coach with us and tried to give us a guided tour round Bucharest in the pitch black! We was not impressed! I've been to hundreds of away games since but that trip is the one that always stands out for me.
Barry Smith, Ellesmere Port.

The journey to Rotterdam for our group, started at the old Swanpool Tavern, in the back room for a bit of a 'lock-in' before heading into town and New Street station. Most of us worked at the old Cincinnati factory on Kingsbury Road and we had about 20 going to the match. At the station, it nearly went sour for me as I'd had a little bit too much to drink and desperately needed the loo. There was no toilet to be found, so I did the next best thing and found a discreet wall to pee against, only to receive a tap on the shoulder from a WPC. She was not amused, and started to take down my particulars! Then I did something really silly and gave a false name, while handing over my passport as proof of ID! That's what drink does to you!

All this time, my mates were getting closer to the train, and I'm seeing my first trip abroad to watch the Villa disappear.

Well the WPC, who was quite pretty as I recall, wrote up the incident in her book, told me I'd be hearing from them at a later date and sent me on my way! Two weeks later, still feeling the warm glow of satisfaction of our win, a letter drops through the letterbox. It's a summons and the pretty WPC has written up my little toilet break as something akin to indecent exposure!

My ex-wife was very understanding (not). She blew a gasket as only (ex) wives can! Anyway giving a false name was an own-goal on my behalf, and I was fined £55. But I did get to Rotterdam!
Chris Wegrzynowski, Birmingham.

I was there in Rotterdam. It was the day before my 24th birthday. My dad having faith we would get to the final, had booked a week's holiday in Holland for him and my mom a few months earlier. I went with my then girlfriend by train and the old Dover-Ostend ferry crossing. Travelling through the night and arriving in the early morning in Rotterdam meant we were able to catch up on sleep in the hotel they were staying at.

There was a game between Villa and Bayern fans on a pitch adjacent to the stadium. I remember we walked past in the afternoon and a few fans were having a kick around into one goal. When we came back later there was a full scale game going on, approximately 100-a-side. I think the 'players' tied a scarf to their arm to show which side they were on, as replica shirts were not so in vogue then. The pitch was surrounded by fans, and it was all very good natured.

We all know the outcome of the game. At the end it occurred to me that just 10 years earlier I had been at a midweek match watching us lose to Torquay United away in the Third Division. That is progress in anybody's book.

We left after the game in my dad's car and it was quite tricky getting a ferry back in the early hours of the morning. We called in at Ostend and Zeebrugge seeing loads of Villa fans milling around and no spaces available on boats. We eventually got on a crossing from Calais, the floor covered with Villa fans everywhere trying to grab a couple of hours' sleep.
Roger Hatfield, Sutton Coldfield, West Midlands.

I was really ill – as it turned out I had pneumonia but that didn't stop me travelling to Rotterdam as I'd waited a long time for something like this. I was still recovering from winning the League the year before. My abiding memories though start at Ostend when we were marched from the ferry to the coaches at gunpoint by the Belgian police. Then some crazy woman went to pat a police dog, it couldn't have gone madder had she squeezed its nuts!

On to Rotterdam and the match. When Peter Withe scored I just pointed my souvenir flag at the sky and yelled daaaaaaaaaaad in memory of my old man who never gave me anything other than the Villa gene. How he would have loved that. The clock at the Bayern end was directly in my eyeline and I can honestly say there was never a longer 25 minutes in my life.

After we got back to Ostend because I was feeling ill I was dying of thirst but you could not get into any bar in town as they were packed with celebrating drunken Villa fans. I said to my mates that I had noticed this place just up the road as we entered town that seemed to be open and we should try there. So we all trooped off (about six of us if I remember correctly) and sure enough it was open, the only problem was it was a knocking shop and the 'lady' of the night on duty couldn't speak English! I tried in my elementary schoolboy French to tell her I was not there for her favours only a drink of water! At this stage her minder came out and showed us the door. I left home on the Monday evening and got back sometime on Thursday night. My football-hating missus was delighted we won and ushered me straight to the doctors.

I still managed to get to town for the homecoming despite feeling like I was at death's door.

Happy days!

Dave Shelley, Birmingham.

Memories From The Holte

Villa Park has seen some great games in the past; and some dire ones as well!

Here are a selection of stories about watching our claret and blue heroes on our own turf.

☉

14 August 1993
Villa 4 Queen's Park Rangers 1

I vividly recall the sounds of my first visit to Villa Park. From the buzz of chatter walking to the ground, to the fanzine sellers calling out from the curbs; from the clicking of the turnstiles to the incredible noise that greeted the teams as they made their way on to the pitch. This was the place I would come to call home.

It was a bright sunny day in August 1993 and Villa hosted Queen's Park Rangers in the opening fixture of the new Premier League season. The previous year we had finished runners-up to Manchester United and the club headed into the new campaign with hope, optimism and confidence. It was

Holte Enders celebrating a goal scored for Villa. It is special scoring at the Holte End.

a day of firsts. Not only was it my first match, the Witton Lane Stand had its new upper tier. On the field manager Ron Atkinson had done some rebuilding of his own, with Andy Townsend making his debut following a £2.1 million move from Chelsea, while Gordon Cowans had returned to the club on a free transfer from Blackburn Rovers. Interestingly, it was also the first time squad numbers were used and players wore shirts with their names emblazoned upon them.

The match began in typical new season style. Neither side were instantly fluent and there was some nervous defending. But as new boy Townsend settled in the middle of the park, Villa slowly began to take the game to their opponents and at 38 minutes they opened the scoring with the debut boy instrumental in setting up Dalian Atkinson for the first goal. Townsend came bursting through the midfield and across the halfway line before threading a ball through to Atkinson who just managed to beat onrushing goalkeeper Tony Roberts to the ball. The burly forward was injured in the process but it was a goal he fully deserved.

QPR drew level on the stroke of half-time, the lethal Les Ferdinand taking advantage of some pinball inside the Villa box before lashing home a 25-yard half volley past Nigel Spink into the top right hand corner for a stunning goal.

The second half started much like the first, although Spink was twice forced to save from the continuing threat of Ferdinand. But with almost 60 minutes on the clock, Big Ron decided to change things by introducing Cowans – and it was to prove decisive as Villa regained the lead three minutes later.

Following a six-man move, Dean Saunders cleverly worked an opening on the edge of the box to curve home a right-foot shot into the bottom corner. With Cowans in dominant mood, Villa finally stamped their authority on the game and finished their opponents off in style. Going into stoppage time, Atkinson powered home his second, yet another goal from outside of the box and into the top corner. And then, with the final whistle about to go, Steve Staunton allowed the ball to run across his body on the far left hand side of the area before driving home an absolute blinder to almost blow the roof off the new Witton Lane Stand. It was an incredible finale to an unforgettable day. Win, lose or draw you never forget your first game.

'Dad, can I have a season ticket?'

Mark Jones, Birmingham (Aston Villa employee).

23 December 1970, League Cup semi-final, second leg

Villa 2 Manchester United 0

Watching Villa gives you more ups and downs than a ride at Alton Towers, but when the good times are good they are really good. For all the good memories of half a century of watching the team, two stand out – partly because they were in the dark days of the Third Division, after a decade in which Villa had been truly awful. Relegation is bad, double relegation is worse, and after Tommy Docherty's false dawn left Villa at the bottom of the Second Division with all the money spent, the future looked grim. Vic Crowe, Villa's forgotten hero, could not stop a second relegation.

Villa were now in the Third Division and without any money. The first memory showing that the tide had turned was a fantastic game on 23 December 1970. Docherty's expensive signings had not gelled and Villa had looked a collection of strangers. But Crowe produced a fighting unit and when the team went to play Manchester United in the first leg of the League Cup semi-final, we were prepared to give any team a game – even one which had won the European Cup only two and a half years earlier.

A fighting 1–1 draw made the neutrals sit up as Andy Lochhead cancelled out a Brian Kidd goal – Kidd, the same man who is now second in charge at Manchester City, and a great player. But Villa's defence held the United attack to set up one of the all time great games.

The return leg at Villa Park was a sell out, which meant 62,500 people packed into the ground and to be honest very few expected Villa to do it. Looking at the team sheets showed internationals against journeymen for the most part. And things looked bad when mid way through the first half, that man Kidd scored a superb goal at the Witton End in front of his own supporters (until recently, the opposing side supporters were behind the Witton End goal. In those days there was no North Stand). But this was two days before Christmas and Santa Claus was about to arrive.

It was at this point with the Villa staring down the barrel of a gun that the crowd took over. The noise from cheering Villa fans rose to ear splitting levels. It was not just the Holte End. In the Trinity Road stand where I was watching, the crowd in the upper tier began banging their feet on the old wooden floorboards. It was like hearing an express train arriving or an army on the march. Manchester United visibly wilted under the tidal wave of Villa chanting and when veteran Andy Lochhead, the old balding eagle, escaped high priced defender Ian Ure to head a cross from centre-half into the back of the net, the noise level rocketed. The photo shows Ian Ure was facing his own goal as Andy headed the ball. The whole United team was now at sixes and sevens.

The atmosphere was by now electric and no one could hear the United supporters in the Witton End. The crowd and the team were now one fighting unit, but only eleven could be on the pitch and could the Villa lads sustain the pressure? They could! In that second half no team in the world could have lived with the Villa lads, everyone of whom was playing the game of their life. In the 73rd minute came the moment, came the man. The much underrated Villa inside forward Pat McMahon leapt to meet a cross from the right with United centre-half David Sadler in no man's land.

Pat was perfectly balanced, three feet off the ground headed the ball like a bullet past the United goal keeper.

The last 20 minutes were hysterical. The noise was physical, no one had any throat left by the end of the game but when the final whistle went Villa were back at Wembley and we had our self respect back. It was all the more astonishing given that a month earlier Villa had lost in the first round of the FA Cup to Torquay United 3–1. How Vic Crowe had motivated his team is a mystery, but not for the first time Villa showed they could rise to the challenge of the big fish, if not always to bread and butter matches.

A week later Man United sacked manager Wilf McGuinness and put Matt Busby back in charge. It was the start of a long period when they would not be major players in the game. Nor did the result guarantee that the tide had turned for the Villa. Away from Villa Park, we were easily defeated by Spurs in the Final who beat us 2–0. But at least we were no longer in free fall as we had been for a decade.

Many years later, Michael Crick, journalist, and Alex Ferguson's biographer, told me that he had been on the Witton End that night as a 12-year-old Man United supporter experiencing his first away match. He recalled the amazing atmosphere and magnificent old style stadium, but above all the agony of defeat. He left before the end of the game in tears, straight after the McMahon goal, as he knew United would not come back. And for that we have to thank the crowd, who lifted the players to heights they did not know they could play.

Trevor Fisher, Stafford, Staffordshire.

Trevor is the author of *Villa for England*, published by DB Publishing.

26 April 1975
Villa 2 Sunderland 0

My outstanding memory of going to Villa Park was the last home game of the 1974–75 season against Sunderland, watched by a massive crowd of over 57,000. We had to win to get back into the 'big time.' Our rivals in the promotion race were Norwich and Sunderland but even if Sunderland had won, I don't think they could have made second place. It was 0–0 at half-time and people around us were saying 'we're going to miss out if we don't score soon.' We were standing in the lower half of the Trinity Road Stand, near the dug-out and in the second half, we all chanted towards Ron Saunders, 'Bring on Gidman, bring on Gidman...' Eventually, around the hour mark I think, he must have heard us and on came John Gidman and he seemed to change the game. For some reason, with the big crowd behind him, Gidman seemed to have inspired the team to victory.

Scenes showing the pitch invasion after the Villa v Sunderland game on 26 April 1975 after Villa gain promotion back to Division One.

Throughout the game, the PA announcer gave the crowd updates from the other teams involved in the promotion race, like Norwich and Manchester United. So, when the final whistle went we already knew were had been promoted and the PA announcer kindly asked the crowd not to invade the pitch, but inventively, it seemed like all 57,000 people engulfed the pitch, including me. Very quickly, the green turf was completely covered by the hordes of fans celebrating our promotion back to the First Division.

Fred McGreggor, Rugby, Warwickshire.

This game was, I think, more or less a formality. Villa only had to draw, or not lose by a bagful of goals to get promoted from the Second Division and a post-match celebration had been advertised on TV and in local newspapers. So I decided to take my camera along, a Chinon compact camera with a fixed 50mm lens that I'd been given the preceding Christmas. Normally I didn't take the camera for fear of it being broken or stolen. It was a nice day and I probably arrived quite early to bag my spot which was good as the stadium was packed – over 57,000 attended, I believe. The match was quite good, as I recall, with both sides playing competitive football: the final scoreline of 2–0 to the Villa sealed the promotion and was the cue for fans to spill onto the pitch, with the police making no attempt to stop them. That's probably what I will remember most about that day, the grass disappearing under a sea of humanity as everyone faced the Trinity

The crowds died down after the Villa v Sunderland game on 26 April 1975.

Road stand, waiting for manager Ron Saunders and the team to appear. After what seemed an eternity they came out and Ron gave a speech. The atmosphere was fantastic, to this day I've never experienced anything like it. Eventually the crowd began to disperse but I hung around, taking photos of the ground to add to those I'd taken earlier. Limited by the fixed 50mm lens, I even managed to get some decent action shots, although I had to wait for the play to come up quite close to the Witton End touchline! I celebrated my 15th birthday two days later – what a present!

Although I don't attend matches anymore I still follow the Villa and listen out for their results, smiling when they win and groaning when they lose. I still have a claret and blue scarf knitted by my nan, one end of which is covered in sew-on badges. I used to wear it knotted around my neck with the badges proudly on show. Happy days!

Kevin Pitt, Walsall, West Midlands.

5 May 2001

Aston Villa 3 Coventry City 2

I woke up looking forward to the final home game of the season yet at the same time dreading three months without being able to watch my Villa. The sun was shining and the pressure was on Coventry. Well, simple really. Coventry had to win to stay in the Premier League.

We finally arrived at Villa Park after going to the pub (I was a child at the time so didn't drink) I remember just how electric the atmosphere was inside the ground. It was a West Midlands derby that meant so much more to the fans from Coventry.

Soon to be Villa player Mustapha Hadji gave Coventry a two goal lead after grabbing a pair of goals. Things looked up for the Sky Blues and their fans, but then on the hour mark their young 'rookie' goalkeeper at the time, Chris Kirkland made a error by making a save and pushing the ball into the feet of Darius Vassell who slotted home to make it 2–1.

The atmosphere in Villa Park was tense but at the same time incredible. Villa continued to press with David Ginola playing fantastically well and before long Gareth Southgate crossed the ball and Juan Pablo Angel scored his first goal for the club to make it 2–2. And to stick the knife in Villa were awarded a free-kick with Paul Merson hitting a absolute peach into the back of the net.

It felt so wonderful to be a Villa fan that day, not just because we relegated our rivals but because the atmosphere was incredible.

Stuart Young, Birmingham.
Chairman of www.avillafan.com

11 January 1997
Villa 2 Newcastle United 2

It was the year that Newcastle went 10 points clear at the top of the Premier League and we were also doing well. Newcastle went 2–0 up and as fans do, I was shouting at the players. I stood on my seat waving my arms around like a lunatic and accidently hit the chap standing up in front of me over the head with my arms. I realised what I had done and immediately apologised to him, calmed down and started to behave myself somewhat. We got a goal back before half-time through Dwight Yorke and shortly after the break we levelled through Savo Milosevic. Then we got a penalty. Everyone around me was going hysterical. Me and my mate Danny both fell over in the isle when the penalty was awarded and the chap in front of us who I had whacked over the head some time before started hugging us. Typically, the penalty was missed! However, it was one of those games you'll never forget, even though we didn't quite do enough to win the game. Typical Villa!

Shaun McDermott, Sutton Coldfield, West Midlands.

10 January 1948
Villa 4 Manchester United 6

I lived in Walsall as a nipper and I used to cycle from home to The Bell pub on the Birmingham Road, where I would park up my bike and then catch a bus to Perry Barr and walk to Villa Park from there. It was a bit of a long winded way but I didn't go to every game in those days. I was about 12 when Villa played Manchester United in the FA Cup third round in 1948. We were 5–1 down at half-time and somehow got back to lose 6–4. I stood in the Witton stand for that game and after the match I remember I got caught up in the crowds walking down the grass bank; it was dangerous in those days. I was only 'knee high to a grasshopper.' I got carried down the bank, took through the gents toilet and lifted through the window just to get out of the ground. During the process of getting out of the ground I lost one of my shoes so I had to do that journey home with one shoe on and one shoe off.

Barry Riley, Aldridge, Staffordshire.

22 March 2008
Villa 0 Sunderland 1

I went to watch Villa play Sunderland on a freezing cold Saturday afternoon in 2008. I sat in the Trinity Road stand, by the players' tunnel, waiting, pulse racing, eyes sharpened for a polished performance that would sink Roy Keane's Premier League pretenders.

To my horror and to the demise of my extremities (did I mention it was cold?), I watched as Craig Gardner gave the most inept performance at right back I have ever seen. I was so close to him I could almost grab him to make an enforced substitution but my feet, frozen to a piece of 'Hubba Bubba' would not allow me. 'Damn you Craig!' I roared passionately, 'it's only Stephen Reid, he looks like a fat hamster!'

The game was drawing to a close: A pint was waiting to forget this bore draw when, no! This proved too much to ask as Michael Chopra outpaced the Villa defence to lift a cute finish over the onrushing Thomas Sorensen. The Sunderland fans went wild, Craig dropped his head in shame and I swiftly went home.

Three years later, two entirely different Sunderland and Villa teams played out exactly the same game, with, as it turns out, another home reverse. Maybe I was a little hard on young Craig.

David Callaghan, Moseley, Birmingham.

21 February 1972
Villa 2 Santos 1

Brazilian side Santos, including the great Pelé, were touring Europe in 1971–72. My dad and I sat near the front, in the (then) new seats on the Trinity Road lower level (you see I remember this being terracing). I don't remember much of the match but thought Pelé was disappointing. Again the match sticks in my memory for trouble I'm afraid. Because there were no visiting supporters, fans in the Holte End were singing against each other, the 'right' side taking on the 'left' side. I don't know if there was any physical violence.

Kevin Pitt, Walsall, West Midlands.

28 August 2004
Villa 4 Newcastle United 2

This game I will always remember for several reasons, one being the most amazing comeback I have witnessed at Villa Park. It was when Craig Bellamy was playing for Newcastle and when they scored the opener, he paraded up the touchline, near where me and my daughter were sitting, kissing his badge and winding all the Villa fans up. Sometime later Newcastle went 2–0 up but just before half-time, Olof Melburg scored to give us a lifeline. However, my daughter had a party to go to so we had to leave. As we were walking out of the stadium and approached the exit door I asked my daughter, 'do you really want to go to the party? This game could be good.' She turned round to me and replied, 'no dad I want to stay here.' We went back to our seats and watched the remainder of the match. We won 4–2 and I will always remember the Villa fans singing at the end, 'Bellamy what's the score?....' He couldn't even look up as he walked off the pitch. His reaction at the end made it a special match for me.

Danny Drewry, Sutton Coldfield, West Midlands.
www.midlandsmemorablia.com

23 December 1970, League Cup semi-final, second leg,
Villa 2 Manchester United 0

I remember the 1970–71 League Cup semi-final beating Man United 2–1 at Villa Park after drawing the first leg 1–1 at Old Trafford. We were in the Third Division then and they had Best, Law and Charlton. 62,500 in the ground with Lochhead and Pat McMahon scoring for Villa. We probably performed better in the first game but for the sheer unadultered passion, emotion and excitement beating the might of Man United to get to the Final – this was my favourite game ever.

Roger Hatfield, Sutton Coldfield, West Midlands.

It ranks with the 5–1 Liverpool win in 1970 as one of the great Villa Park nights of my life. I'd failed to get a ticket but on the day before the game I travelled up from Redditch to Birmingham to do Christmas shopping and word spread around the city that Manchester United had returned some

Pat McMahon puts Villa in the lead against Manchester United on 23 December 1970.

of their tickets. I went straight to Villa Park and queued for a couple of hours to get my ticket. Even 40 years on my memories of the game are still fresh and I'll never forget the Holte going berserk when Pat McMahon scored the winner.

Frank Smith, Horsham, West Sussex.

All those years have passed and there hasn't been much to match that occasion. It may be a view through nostalgia but I have always looked back on that night with great memories.

The headline read simply, 'HEADS IT'S ANDY'.

John P Knibb, Birmingham.

A fantastic night – certainly the biggest crowd (62,500) I'd been in up until then. I'd been going to matches for two years by then and had been more used to crowds around the 20,000 mark when you could pick your spot to stand in. I can to this day see in my mind's eye the ball coming off Andy's head for the equaliser at the Holte End and Pat McMahon's diving header at the Witton. This may have been a Manchester United side on the slide but they still had the likes of Law, Best and Charlton, so not a bad achievement for a Third Division side. Happy Days!

Bernie Moore, Bristol.

17 March 1998
Villa 2 Atletico Madrid 1

Of all the ones I have attended, my favourite game was the Atletico Madrid home game. It had everything, and when Collymore scored, I remember

me and my mate looking at one another in total disbelief before crying with utter joy, and bearhugging the two massive skinheads behind us in the Witton Lane. We were right next to the Atletico fans and we spent the whole game singing and chanting. I remember quite clearly thinking that it was the happiest I've ever been.
Mick Coles, Walsall, West Midlands.

12 February 1972
Villa 2 Bournemouth 1

We were still in the Third Division, and the crowd could not raise us for a promotion push that season. But in the second awful year in what is now League One (but really is the Third Division) Vic Crowe had to deliver a miracle. A huge club with huge support but playing clubs like Wrexham and Chesterfield. It was not an easy ask and when we played our main rivals at home, Bournemouth with a then wonder striker Ted MacDougall, it all looked as though it could go horribly wrong. Ted MacDougall had a diagram put in the mirror of how he scored it, it was his best goal, be good to get that – I long since lost my press cutting.

But we won the match and his brilliance went for nothing – and a transfer to Manchester United.
Trevor Fisher, Stafford, Satffordshire.

Andy Lochhead against Bournemouth in 1972.

23 September 1995
Villa 1 Nottingham Forest 1

One of my best memories is of Andy Townsend against Forest. Townsend scored to put us in the lead and he celebrated by jumping into the fans in the Holte End. Everyone was going crazy but he got booked for his over-elaborate celebration. Straight from the kick-off, Townsend went for the ball with two-feet and missed the ball and for that he got sent off for a second bookable offence. To cap it all, Des Little equalised for Forest in the 94th minute, just as we all thought Villa were marching onto victory. For me it was one of those games you will always remember.

Shaun McDermott, Sutton Coldfield, West Midlands.

12 December 2004
Villa 1 Birmingham City 2

Living in London as I do, the Birmingham derby is still as important to me as ever. However, the match in December 2004 was definitely one to forget. It all started badly when I got up late and had to dash to Euston Station to board the train. Probably my own doing as I had a few drinks the night before, but I blame the alarm clock and I'm sticking to it!

Anyway, I managed to get the train and so off I trotted on my way to Villa Park to what I thought would be a certain victory for the boys in claret and blue. Just before I reached New Street Station, I realised that I had forgotten my mobile phone and so I couldn't call a friend or my old man to pick me up! I usually do this when I arrive on the day of a match, as they can pick me up on the way to the ground. However, as luck would have it, there was a train going to Witton virtually as I arrived at the station, so I wondered over to the platform, still in a bit of a daze and jumped on the train.

Little did I know that the train was only full of Birmingham City supporters and not a Villa fan in sight. You can guess that I had abuse, beer thrown at me, and was slapped a couple of times before we reached Witton Station. I couldn't wait to get off the train and so I ran down the ramp, only to then be greeted by a mob of Villa supporters awaiting the train and the Birmingham City supporters! How could I explain that I was Villa for one, and secondly, I didn't really want to stick around in any case!

So there I was, honestly, stuck in between two angry mobs, one of which had just given me loads of abuse and the other who was about to. Once the

Blues fans got off the train, the two sets clashed and I found myself being punched by all sides on a very thin ramp! Nothing I could do. Once I eventually got out of it, I ran to Villa Park ready for the match and to tell my story to the amusement of my friends and family.

Unfortunately we were beaten 2–1 at home that afternoon too and then I had the long haul home on a delayed and re-routed train which took hours to get back to London. It didn't even go to Euston due to train works and so I ended up in Marylebone, bruised, unhappy and fearing the worst for the Villa.

Not a good day to be had at all and so when the chips are down I often think could it get any worse than that fateful day in 2004?
Matt Walker, London.

14 November 1959
Villa 11 Charlton Athletic 1

Gerry Hitchens was one of my all-time favourites. Would you believe I saw almost every game in the 1959–60 season when Villa won promotion back to the First Division, but one game I missed was the 11–1 victory against Charlton Athletic at Villa Park when Hitchens scored five. I had gone to Spain to attend a friend's wedding. The only consolation was that the day after, I did go to the Nou Camp to see Barcelona in a Spanish League match.

Gerry Hitchens trying to escape the adoring fans after the 11–1 victory on 14 November 1959.

Frank Allen, Droitwich, Worcestershire.

16 January 1943
Villa 3 Stoke City 0

At 74 years of age my Villa memories go back a long way. In fact to the early 1940s when I was taken by my father to Villa Park to see my first ever football match. Looking across Villa Park for the first time from the Witton Lane side, seeing the bomb damaged end of one stand. I think that was probably the Trinity Road stand. Hearing so much noise and seeing so many people, the deafening roar when the Villa team came out of the tunnel. As a six or seven-year-old this was a memory that will stay with me for the rest of my life.

143

I was hooked. This was the day in my young life when I was destined to become a Villa fan forever.

The Villa names that I recall although not sure now if they played on this particular day were:

Goalkeeper Alan Wakeman, full-backs Vic Potts and George Cummings, half-backs, Harry Parkes, 'Mush' Callaghan, Alex Massie (Capt.)

Forwards Frank Broom (outside-right), Ian Haycock, George Edwards, Bob Iverson and of course Eric Houghton (outside-left).

All so different from the positions that the modern day game demands.

Over the next few years I rarely missed a home game until August 1955 when I was called up for National Service.

Ken Toy, Hall Green, Birmingham.

15 December 1976
Villa 5 Liverpool 1

I am pleased to be able to say I was at this game. I was standing in the Witton End of the ground and so had a great view of all the goals. The goal that stood out for me was Brian Little's. He had the ball on the edge of the penalty area on the Witton Lane side of the ground, looked up, saw Clemence off his line and curled a beautiful shot into the top corner of the net. The other thing I clearly remember was Clemence, Hughes and Thompson having a big argument and blaming each other as they walked off at half time while the Villa players had a standing ovation. I Must admit I had forgotten that Jake Findlay and Charlie Young played in that game, both were reserve team players so that made our win even more remarkable.

Steve Poole, Manila, Philippines (formerly from Birmingham)

Up For The Cup!

The 1957 FA Cup Final between Villa and Manchester United was played on 4 May 1957 at Wembley Stadium. As every Villa fan should know, Villa beat the 'Busby Babes' 2–1, with both of their goals scored by Peter McParland. Tommy Taylor scored United's goal.

The Final was marred by a collision after only six minutes between Villa forward Peter McParland and United goalkeeper Ray Wood, which left Wood unconscious with a broken cheekbone. Wood left the pitch and Jackie Blanchflower took over in goal for United.

Villa's victory gave them their seventh FA Cup title, a record number at the time but unfortunately we haven't been able to add to that total since, which has been passed by three clubs.

⚽

Peter McParland talks briefly about his memory of that day.

It was always a dream of mine to reach a FA Cup Final at Wembley (and ultimately to win it). Wembley was a big thing back then as it is today. In 1957 it was not a dream any longer as we got there. It was (and still is) every footballer's dream to score the winning goal in the Cup Final and I lived the dream on that day by scoring a couple of goals and helping the team to win the Cup. My biggest regret is that I did not complete a hat-trick, which would have been something very special, and I still rue the moment I hit the post.

Hearing the final whistle after the Cup Final victory was in stark contrast to hearing the final whistle when we were relegated at The Hawthorns two years later. Rather than my heart sinking to the floor, I stood in the middle of the Wembley pitch in total amazement that we had won it. It took a wee bit of time to sink in and I don't think it became reality until we walked up those steps to lift the trophy.

Peter McParland, former Villa forward 1952–62.

Ray Graydon signed for Bristol Rovers before making a £50,000 move to Aston Villa in July 1971. He immediately helped them to the Third Division title. After Ron Saunders replaced Vic Crowe in June 1974, Graydon scored 11 goals in the first 12 League games under the new manager – not bad for a wide man.

Meanwhile, Villa's League Cup trail started to turn those dreams into reality. Saunders' men beat Everton, Crewe, Hartlepool, Colchester and Chester to book a Wembley date with the Canaries.

A cagey Final was clinched by Graydon's goal. Seconds after flirting with ignominy, when goalkeeper Kevin Keelan saved his penalty, the number seven became the hero by netting the rebound. Every piece had

The League Cup Final celebrations in 1974–75 at Wembley.

fitted into place. It was pretty much the perfect day for Ray Graydon, a player and a man whose honesty and decency makes the conduct of many of today's top 'stars' seem even more squalid. Not that, back in 1975, everything went exactly to plan as Ray explains here.

Any youngster that dreamed of being a footballer, as I did, dreamed of playing in a Wembley Final. So when my dream came true I was determined to savour every moment of the day. For me it was not just about the football, it was a wonderful family occasion. My mum and dad, my wife and brothers and sister were there and lots of friends. To score the winner in front of them was an amazing feeling. My mum and dad are gone now, bless them, but I was so happy to have done that when they were there to see it.

I still have very special memories of that day. That night we went to the Savoy Hotel and, after the team meal, and were joined by our families. Doug Ellis bought all the wives a pendant and a bottle of champagne. It was a lovely evening and I remember, right at the end of it, walking in the cul-de-sac outside the Savoy with my family and my father turned to me. 'Well that was a bloody great day'. I was amazed. I said, 'dad, I've never heard you swear before', and he said, 'son, if you are ever lucky enough to have a son and he goes on to play for a big club in a Wembley Final and scores the winning goal in front of 100,000, then I think you'll swear.'

One of my dreams was to be in the victory lap of honour round the stadium, but somebody pulled me through the fence that was round the ground in those days and by the time I got going again the rest of the players had left me behind. I couldn't catch up. I was last back in the dressing room but that gave me another memory that will never fade. It was a big communal bath, big enough to swim in, and all the other players had gone so I was on my own. There were cardboard cups of champagne still around and I just swam around with one, taking the day in.

When Chris Nicholl got that header in I started to celebrate but then Mel Machin handballed it and suddenly I thought 'Hey up, it's me now'. Kevin made a good save, although I was quite happy with the kick I'd taken, but luckily the ball fell back to me and I stuck it in. Mel lives in Bournemouth now and I'm in Eastleigh so we still see each other and play golf from time to time. I'm still in touch with Chris too.

It was a wonderful day and I'll always be grateful I was lucky enough to be part of it. Cup Finals are great occasions and, if you win, leave a lot of great memories whether you play or watch.

Ray Graydon, former Villa winger 1971–77

In 1957, the year to always remember, Villa won the FA Cup playing against Manchester United. I well remember risking the wrath of a Sgt Major as I sneaked out of my office every 15 minutes or so to check on the score in the semi-final replay when Villa were playing the Albion at St Andrews.

When that day arrived, 4 May 1957, I had no chance of getting to Wembley but I had to race to get home to Birmingham and watch the game on a little black and white television. The result is now history, but among my most treasured souvenirs are my copies of the *Sports Argus* proclaiming 'CLARET AND BLUE CUP', and also the *Birmingham Mail* Sports Final printed in claret and blue with three inch headlines 'VILLA`S CUP.'

On the return journey to Manchester the next day it was agreed by about 15 of my Brummie pals that when we walked down the platform of Manchester's London Road Station (now Manchester Piccadilly) at about 2 am and much to the annoyance of lots of Manchester rail porters we would all be chanting 'Villa'.

Ken Toy, Hall Green, Birmingham.

My greatest memory is of the 1957 FA Cup Final and watching Peter McParland score those two goals to beat Manchester United at Wembley. To this day, I say it was a fair challenge on their goalkeeper Ray Wood. No question about it!!

Eric Johnson, Hednesford, Staffordshire.

In 1957 I saw the Villa beat Manchester United at Wembley and was accompanied by a very good school friend, Malcolm Smith. We watched the infamous occasion when Peter McParland floored Ray Wood and then went on to score the two winning goals; however, my friend, Malcolm, emigrated to Australia a few years later.

Since he emigrated all those years ago, I have seen my friend Malcolm only twice but in August 2011, I am flying out to Sydney to spend a few weeks with him. We are also popping over to New Zealand to watch a couple of World Cup Rugby games. So 54 years after THE Cup win, I will be seeing my match companion once again and more importantly, meeting the man who was responsible in the main, for winning the trophy.
Pete Haden, Aston Villa tour guide.

When I was 10 my mother took me and my younger brother to meet the Villa players at Lewis's in Birmingham before the 1957 FA Cup Final. There was a long table with all the Villa players sat in a line signing their Pre-Cup Final Players Handbook, except for one player who would be stood at a microphone talking to the fans.

Mom bought me the handbook and I moved along with the players signing the team photo on the back cover.

Nigel Sims and Jimmy Dugdale were my favourites and I was determined to shake their hands. As luck would have it they were sat next to each other. Jimmy signed for me and I sheepishly put out my hand, Jimmy said 'no son the pen is mine', I mumbled something like, 'shake' and Nigel, next in line, guessed what I was trying to do and said, 'the wee fellow wants to shake hands'. Jimmy smiled and shook my hand and I shook hands with Nigel and carried on just getting the other players' signatures. I remember hearing another boy say, 'look mom he's shaking hands'. And when I looked back after I had got my book fully signed all the other kids were shaking hands with all the players. I bet I was not too popular.

Peter McParland was the only one I did not get as he was on the microphone as I went along the line. I still have the handbook, my most treasured Villa item.
Robert Dore, Ettington, Stratford-Upon-Avon, Warwickshire.

Born in south Birmingham, I have been supporting the Villa for nearly 60 years and moved to Australia four years ago, but in the sixties and seventies was working in the theatre and TV professionally.

In 1975 I was appearing at The Victoria Palace Theatre in London with Max Bygraves (another Villa connection as he was also a supporter due to his close friendship with Harry Parkes). Max, knowing of my support, asked, one day if I fancied going with him to Wembley for the LCF against Norwich. (Harry P. would not be going and we could have his tickets).

There was only one problem! We had two shows to do on a Saturday and as the first one was at 6pm we would have to leave before the final whistle. He would arrange, however, for his driver to be waiting right outside Wembley to rush us to Victoria. Needless to say the seats were great, right next to the Royal Box, but the game was not the greatest. (I had memories of 1971 and the disappointment at seeing us lose to Spurs). It was still 0–0 when we had to leave.

We got outside the stadium and there was a big roar which quickly died (obviously not a goal), all quiet for a few moments then chanting which then died down (no idea which fans were cheering), then a huge 'oooh', a moments quiet and a huge roar. Frustratingly for us not a clue as to what had happened! Just then the car arrived and the driver was able to tell us that Villa had a penalty, Ray Graydon had hit the post but had scored from the rebound. (Suddenly the cheers above made sense!).

Needless to say the shows that night were performed on a real high, although I had to wait till the next day to actually see the goal.

Des Farmer, Maroochydore, Queensland, Australia.

I was at Wembley at the Cup Final (1957) against Manchester United and sat behind the goal with a big bell!! What a game. I have it on DVD and love watching until this day. I also attended a dance at Egbaston Reservoir not long after the Cup Final and Johnny Dixon, Villa's Captain announced on the mike that, 'WE STILL WOULD HAVE WON!' as there was only 10 men for United. Also at the dance were a number of Albion players' including England International Derek Kevan.

Trevor Heath, Solihull, West Midlands.

I arrived at Wembley a little worse for wear with a few of my mates; one had a broken hand following a scuffle with a Leeds fan. When we got into the stadium I fell asleep almost immediately as soon as I sat down. The next thing I knew I was awoken by one of my mates, Phil O'Malley, who was shaking me and screaming, 'Savo's scored...' I jumped out of my seat and started jumping up and down. I remember everyone around me was going crazy and hugging each other.

It turned out to be a great day and my abiding memory of it was at the end the whole of the Villa end singing, 'it's up to you Dwight Yorke, Dwight Yorke....' Great day.

Shaun McDermott, Sutton Coldfield, West Midlands.

It was 1971 and in those days jelly and ice cream or jelly and blancmange for Sunday tea was the norm in most households and Chivers was the best known manufacturer of jelly. That year Villa reached the League Cup Final at Wembley and we all set off with high expectations of beating Spurs. Sitting on the train home barely anybody spoke a word until a guy in our carriage broke the silence with the immortal words, 'I will never eat another bloody jelly as long as I live'. Confused? – Martin Chivers scored both goals in our 2–0 defeat.

Paul Farrington, Halesowen, West Midlands.

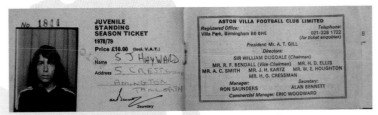

How things used to be. A juvenile season ticket for Aston Villa 1978–79.

I recently dug out my old season ticket from 1978–79 and a photo of myself from the early 1970s wearing a Villa kit of the time. It doesn't have a badge, and there were no numbers or names available to put on the back of the shirt and of course no sponsors on the front. I cannot remember many kids having replica football shirts or kits back then, but what I do remember is my nan giving me my Uncle Paul's (my Nan's son)

Simon Hayward from Tamworth shows off his (early 1970s) Villa football kit. Notice there were no shirt sponsors on the kit.

football socks because I did not have any. The only problem being that Paul, unlike anyone else in the family, was a Birmingham City supporter and they were blue and white socks (as you can see in the photo). This did not bother me as I was still very proud to have a Villa kit. My uncle, Paul Hayward went on to have a very successful career in non League football during the 1970s and 1980s playing for the likes of Hednesford Town, Atherstone United, Stourbridge, Nuneaton Borough and with Tamworth in the 1980s. I really admired Paul and he was my mentor, but he never persuaded me to be a City fan!

I was not allowed to go and see the Villa until around the mid-1970s, because of my parents' fear of some of the violence and trouble that would often occur at football matches in those days. When I did go it was with another uncle, my Uncle Arthur, who was a big Villa fan, but he would often leave going to the match until the last minute which would lead to a fast drive from Kingstanding to the ground in his Mini and then trying to park as close to the ground as possible. A few of the times we would go into the away end because it was quicker to get into the ground and back out again. This I found quite frightening as I had to hide my scarf and try not to speak in case the other fans heard my accent, especially as we were all tightly squashed together standing on the terraces.

I can remember a few times when trouble did occur, usually outside the ground. On one occasion I can remember lots of wild and very aggressive Chelsea fans who had all just come out of the ground onto Witton Lane being held back by police who had their arms linked together trying to stop them attacking Villa fans as they walked past. Scary stuff!

By 1978–79 (aged 15) I had my own season ticket and was now going to the ground by myself, catching the bus from Tamworth where I lived to the ground and back again. The Holte End was where I went and there was no more going in the away end!

My most memorable match that season was 16 April 1979 when we beat Liverpool 3–1. I can remember one of the goals going straight through Ray Clemence's legs, Ray was a great keeper so this made it all the more memorable, but Liverpool did go on to win the title that year. It was also the same day that day that I met Gordon Cowans at Belgrave in Tamworth. It was the presentation night for Belgrave Albion, the football club that I played for. This was a great honour for me and I can remember sitting next to him and his girlfriend talking about the Liverpool game!!

Simon Hayward, Tamworth, Staffordshire.

At the beginning of 1996 Aston Villa were still going strong in all competitions. In the League Cup Brian Little's team had handed a heavy

6–0 defeat to Peterborough United and managed to see off Stockport County and Queens Park Rangers before being drawn against local rivals Wolverhampton Wanderers in the quarter-finals. Villa had been drawn at home in all the previous rounds and it was to be our advantage again for what would be a loud and passionate January night at Villa Park.

I have never looked forward to derby games and it all stems from this match. I grew up in the Black Country and was still at secondary school, so the thought of losing to Wolves just didn't bear thinking about. Promotion hopefuls at the start of the season, Wolves were struggling in the League and manager Mark McGee had recently replaced former England and Villa manager Graham Taylor at Molineux. His first four games had failed to yield a victory, though Wolves had shown they were capable of causing an upset having beaten Coventry City in the previous round. Even so, the omens were good for Villa. Wolves had never beaten us in the competition, but fans of both clubs knew it would be a close game with Wolves having nothing to lose and the pressure being on us to attack.

In a tense first half Villa dominated possession but the play rarely entered their penalty area. Villa were restricted to hopeful long-range shots and it took Wolves half an hour to register their first effort on goal, Steve Bull testing Mark Bosnich at his near post. Five minutes later a 40-yard Darren Ferguson pass found Don Goodman but he could only slice the ball wide. Those were two good chances for Wolves but four minutes before the break Villa had one of their own, Alan Wright crossing to an unmarked Savo Milosevic, who headed wide. All square in a tight first half.

After the interval it was Wolves applying the pressure, Alan Wright was involved at the other end this time, twice clearing off the line from corners before Goodman hit the outside of a post. A deflected Mark Rankine effort also had Bosnich worried. It was becoming unbearable to watch but Villa rediscovered their composure, creating chances for Andy Townsend, who hit the side netting and Dwight Yorke, who headed over the bar. Then, in the 66th minute, a Dwight Yorke through ball released the overlapping Gary Charles who crossed to the unmarked Tommy Johnson.

Steaming into the six-yard box, Johnson volleyed in off goalkeeper Mike Stowell

Dwight Yorke, Savo Milosevic and Ian Taylor with the League Cup Trophy in 1996.

into the corner of the net. The noise that greeted the goal immense; pandemonium struck the Holte End and the relief was euphoric. We had finally unlocked the stubborn Wolves defence! Despite struggling for confidence in the League, Wolves refused to lie down and an anxious 20 minutes remained. McGee changed things in search of a goal to take the tie to a reply and it almost brought one in the final moments when Bull tested Bosnich twice with a header and then the follow up.

The final whistle came not a moment too soon. We had squeezed through and Villa headed for a record breaking ninth semi-final appearance in the League Cup. The rest is history. Aston Villa went on to beat Arsenal on away goals over two legs after coming from two-down in the first leg at Highbury. Then in the final against Leeds United at Wembley an emphatic 3–0 victory crowned an excellent season for the club. But that tense quarter-final against Wolves is the game which sticks in my mind...

Mark Jones, Birmingham (Aston Villa employee).

Villa in Verse

I find it quite ironic that football fans shout all sorts of things during the game, and you always hear some funny stuff, but getting them to stand up and speak in front of an audience or write it down on paper is another matter all together. Poetry about football is not such a daft idea when you think about it. After all aren't the songs that have traditionally been sung up and down the nation's terraces a form of urban poetry?

Football chants are considered to be accessible, irreverent, funny and sometimes quite beautiful (but unfortunately, sometimes distasteful). If you have visited Villa Park over the last 40 years or so, you would have heard a chorus or two sounding something like, 'He's claret, he's blue. He scores a goal or two. Agbonlahor! Agbonlahor!' or 'Gary Shaw, Gary Shaw, Gary, Gary Shaw. He hits the ball and bound to score, Gary, Gary Shaw...' That's about as poetic as most football fans get and there's hundreds more songs along the same lines about different footballers or managers who have passed through the club over the years.

World-renowned, self-styled 'football poets' have grown in numbers and profile over the years and there are even websites dedicated entirely, would you believe, to football poetry. In the past 15 years people have become more and more confident in wielding the pen and publishing their work or performing their 'football in verse' in public. Poetry is a way of self-expression but it can also be inspirational too; however, poetry is still seen in some circles to be a bit pretentious and bourgeois and some poets may be perceived as eccentric but the new wave of football poetry has gone a long way to change that theory.

This chapter of the book is meant to be a bit different and a way of introducing poetry to you, the fans. It may not be everyone's cup of tea, but I am sure when you read the pieces of work in the coming pages, you will appreciate the sentiments and relive some of the moments which have been captured in verse. I have sourced some excellent pieces from the very best poets, including a former Poet Laureate, several nationally recognised children's poets (who happen to be Villa fans) and a self-styled football poet, as well as several from Villa fans.

Enjoy!!

✪

The Night Villa Ruled Europe
By Emdad Rahman

De Kuip in swanky Rotterdam
In town Karl-Heinz Rummenigge
Villa's claret face Bavarian might
Mortimer locks horns with Breitner
Old hand Withe pairs young Shaw
Opposing Hoeness and Augenthaler
Morley rampant on the wing
Cowans is chief playmaker
'Shaw, Williams prepared to venture down the left,'
Brian Moore through gritted teeth
'There's a good ball played in for Tony Morley!
Oh it must be! And it is! Peter Withe!'

Brum's on seats as the Villains hang on
Hand shook with Artemio Franchi
Mortimer lifts such glistening silver
Barton's men make Villa history
Rimmer now a champion twice
It's now six years in a row
Europe bows to English rule
Where the claret and blue rivers flow
Spink, Swain, McNaught,
Evans, Williams, Rimmer,
Cowans, Bremner, Withe,
Shaw, Morley, Mortimer

© **Emdad Rahman 2011.**
Emdad Rahman, East London.

Born and bred in the UK, Emdad Rahman refers to himself as a 'novice football poet'. He is a civil servant in London and his latest book is called, 'The Great Game on Earth – A Collection of Fooballing Verse.'
www.football-poems.com
www.tsu-doh-nimh.blogspot.com

When Dennis Went Up For The Cup
By Doug O'Brien

Signed in '75
To give our midfield drive
He was Saunders's inspiration.
A paragon of class
With pedigree to last

He was an absolute Villa sensation.
Imperious in style
He ran mile after mile
Determined his team wouldn't fail.
This leader of men
Proved time and again
That his quality and strength would prevail.

A true Villa boy
Brought us Championship joy
Restoring our pride and our glory.
But this true sentiment
And this true testament
Only tells half of the story!
For in Rotterdam in '82
When all our dreams came true

As Dennis ascended those Stairs.
Yes, when Dennis, went up
To lift the European Cup
We were there
WE WERE THERE!

© **Doug O'Brien.**
Doug O'Brien (Villa fan), Erdington, Birmingham.

Dark Side of the Isle – Paul McGrath
By Emdad Rahman

Thrown out by Fergie
Became a Holte End hero
Beckoned the knackers yard
And McGrath hit minus zero

Curse the dreaded bottle
Suppressed by the Villa Park reign
Irish cordiality meant he'd never
Have to pay for a Guinness again

An Orphan from St Patrick's
Two World Cups and Euro eighty eight
Esteem of a million fans
For the all-time Irish great

© **Emdad Rahman**
Emdad Rahman, East London

One Ian Taylor
By Doug O'Brien

One Ian Taylor
There's only one Ian Taylor!
Every fan knew
We could rely upon you

When you played in the great Villa side.
Always true to the claret & blue
He wore his Villa shirt with pride.

From box to box
He'd work off his socks
Sheer poetry in motion.
Intercept a pass
Cover every blade of grass
And tackle 'em like a Trojan.

So versatile
And he played with a smile
He'd run & he'd chase all day.
Winning the wars
Fighting our cause
With a gritty and determined display.

From Centre Midfield
Many victories were sealed
He scored many vital goals..
In this position
He was a man on a mission
And he played many starring roles.

MEMORIES MADE IN ASTON

In living the dream
For his great boyhood team
Comes this remarkable story.
So picture the scene
Out on Wembley's plush green
And it's destinies moment of glory.

For it's Villa v Leeds
When the great man succeeds
In an image I'll never forget.
'Tayls' wheeling away
On that glorious day
And the ball's in the back of the net.

And the mark of the man
Ask any Villa fan
Came the day when 'Tayls' was banned
Cos to no one's surprise
Shouting 'Up The Villa Boys!'
It's Ian Taylor in the stand!

And right to this day
If you're down Witton way
A special chant's heard without failure.
Both to honour the past
And acknowledge the class
Of the legendary 'One Ian Taylor!'
One Ian Taylor
There's only one Ian Taylor!

© Doug O'Brien.
Doug O'Brien (Villa fan), Erdington, Birmingham.

A New Club Crest
By Doug O'Brien

Villa invest in a new Club crest
We wear it proudly on our chest.
Embroidered with precision
This marvellous exhibition
And demonstrates the clear intent
Of Randy's Villa vision.

Heraldically designed
AVFC enshrined
It captivates our hearts
And encapsulates our minds.
Upholding our tradition
It states with clear ambition

We're chartering a course
For the Champions League mission.
And everybody's wowed
'Cos the lion stands proud
Confirming unanimity
In uniting all the crowd.

And so the star shines bright
We recall that special night
Of European triumph
As The Villa scaled the heights!
With no expenses spared
The motto reads 'PREPARED'

For each and every challenge
And experience to be shared.
Symbolic in constitution
Significant in contribution
Signalling the hopes and dreams
Of Randy's revolution.

And stated clearly
Is its message plain to see
Welcome everybody
To the 'Villa Family'.

© **Doug O'Brien.**
Doug O'Brien (Villa fan), Erdington, Birmingham.

I'm Just a Girl
By Jade Elizabeth Barber

I'm just a girl
Who loves to wear claret and blue
And I don't care what people say

As I'm just a fan
Who lives in London
And I support a northern team
The bells are ringing for claret and blue
The bells are singing for claret and blue
Everybody is knowing
To the Villa we're going
'Cos the Villa are showing
We're the best in the land
Claret and blue.
I wear my claret and blue shirt with pride
'Cos I'm just a fan
And I'm Villa till I die.

© **Jade Elizabeth Barber.**
Jade Elizabeth Barber (Villa fan), Edmonton, London.

There were a lot of poetry written in the Wipers Times (a trench magazine that was published by soldiers fighting on the front lines of the First World War) and some of it was quite good. Sadly, it was almost invariably anonymous, but this one was published in November 1917 (at which time it was the BEF Times). It says something to me about the British front line soldier and what made him so resilient. Note the Villa connection.

The Burning Question
By an unknown First World War soldier

Three 'Tommies' sat in a trench one day
Discussing the war, in the usual way
They talked of the mud, and they talked of the 'Hun'
Of what was to do, and what had been done.
They talked about rum, and – 'tis hard to believe –
They even found time to speak about leave.
But the point which they argued from post back to pillar
Was whether Notts County could beat Aston Villa.

The night sped away, and zero drew nigh
Equipment made ready, all lips getting dry
And watches consulted with each passing minute
Till five more to go, then 't'would find them all in it
The word came along down the line to 'get ready!'
The sergeants admonishing all to keep steady
But out rang a voice getting shriller and shriller
'I tell yer Notts County can beat Aston Villa!'

The Earth shook and swayed, and the barrage was on
As they leapt o'er the top with a rush and were gone
Away into 'Hunland', through mud and through wire
Stabbing and dragging themselves through the mire
No time to heed those who are falling en route
Till, stopped by a strong point, they lay down to shoot
Then, through the din came a voice: 'Say, Jack Miller!
I tell yer Notts County can beat Aston Villa!'

The strong point has gone, and forward they press
Towards their objective, in numbers grown less
They reach it at last, and prepare to resist
The counter-attack which will come through the mist
Of the rain falling steadily; dig and hang on
The word for support back to H.Q. has gone
The air, charge with moment, grows stiller and stiller –
'Notts County's no earthly beside Aston Villa.'

Two 'Blighties', a struggle through mud to get back
To the old A.D.S. down a rough duck-board track
A hasty field dressing, a ride in a car
A wait in a C.C.S., then there they are
Packed side by side in a clean Red Cross train
Happy in hopes to see Blighty again
Still, through the bandages, muffled, 'Jack Miller
I bet you Notts County can beat Aston Villa!'

Villa-nelle
By Celia Warren

If only I could play for Aston Villa
I've got the kit – the claret and the blue
I'd quash the opposition like Godzilla.
Every game would be a real thriller
I'd show them how to score a goal or two
If only I could play for Aston Villa.

The fans would find a nickname like 'Gorilla'
For me, as the pitch became a zoo
I'd quash the opposition like Godzilla.

161

Their goalie would be crying in his pilla'
I'd make him think he hadn't got a clue
If only I could play for Aston Villa.

They'd look at me and say, 'Here comes The Killer,'
Though, I might get showed a red card, that is true
As I quashed the opposition like Godzilla.
But, for now, I'll lick my strawberry and vanilla
Ice-lolly, while I'm waiting in the queue
To see the lads that play for Aston Villa
Quash the opposition like Godzilla.

© **Celia Warren.**
First published in *Football Fever* – John Foster, OUP, 2000

Celia Warren writes poems mainly for children. Her poems and stories have appeared in hundreds of anthologies, and she is a regular contributor to BBC Television and Radio. She is published by a number of educational publishers including Oxford University Press, Scholastic, Pearsons group, Schofield & Sims and Collins Educational.

Celia wrote a poem about her beloved Aston Villa which was read out by fellow Villa fan Dr Carl Chinn in his authentic Brummie accent on BBC Radio WM a while ago. The poem is called 'Villa-nelle'. A 'Villanelle' is a traditional poetic form, whose repeated lines interweave in a similar style to the traditional Italian dance of the same name.

http://celiawarren.wordpress.com/

The Colour's Run
By Edward Phillip Tooker

Did it have to be my Aston Villa shirt?
Sixty quid each that's got to hurt
It bled claret and bloody blue
What's a guy to do !!
White shirts now uniform-ally pink
The boss will kick up a stink
With vivid purple bruises
Not the colour one normally chooses.
Not when one is trying to make a good impression
When stuck inside a world-wide depression

© **Edward Philip Tooker**
Edward Philip Tooker (Villa fan), New Jersey, USA.

The Team In My Head
By David Hart

The team in my head
Still has Houghton and Saunders
And Paul McGrath
And is captained by Townsend.
But this is the new Villa.
Same old ball
Bosnich has it.
'Come on, Yorkey, turn!'
Saint Steve is still here
And young Hendrie
Has the makings of a star.
Southgate sets his eye on the ball
And it's already in the net
Except that it isn't
It's a beach ball he hit
On windy sand.
Is this a mirror
Of our everyday lives
The build-up
The missed chance
Another build-up
Another chance squandered
More build-up
The attack kept at bay
Another build-up
Some forward movement
New expectations,
The pass back
Across, back again, the groan
The build-up
The new expectations
And the move comes to nothing!!
At the other end Bosnich has it
Hendrie shoots over the bar – very close
I wonder what it's like
To be groaned at
By us in our thousands.
We have enlisted
For repeated disappointment
Bosnich has it.

Bosnich is beaten
And is beaten again
But somehow
The ball doesn't go in.
The few trees through the corner gap
Are beginning to green
And beyond them the M6
The world of nowhere
The world of coming from and going to
A perpetual conveyor belt
Bosnich has it.
Southgate keeps making long passes
To where he seemed to imagine
Someone would be.
Bosnich has it.
Then a Southgate pass is exactly right
And Yorke is on to it
The closest yet
And it needs saving.
The crowd is appeased
With such small moments of excitement
Alone in his half of the field
The Bosnich ballet
That is that event called a goal
Will it happen ever again?
Pressure counts
With hindsight
And a deflection is a lucky break
This one is off Joachim -
'The scorer for Aston Villa: Ian Taylor!'
Bosnich flies along the ground
And punches the ball away
And before long again
We are all on our feet
And the ball
In a blur
Is in the net: Yesssssss!
'For Aston Villa's No.9, Savo Milosovic!'

© **David Hart.**
David Hart, Kings Heath, Birmingham.

David Hart was Birmingham Poet Laureate between 1997 and 1998. He is an avid Villa fan and has written some poems specifically about Villa and he has allowed me to share them for this book. He was born and grew up in Aberystwyth but spent most of his life in Birmingham and was Birmingham Poet Laureate, during which time David wrote more Birmingham poems than he had before. During that period he asked the then Villa Chairman, Doug Ellis, for tickets to bring his then young children to a match, and offered to write something for him. He obliged and David sent Mr Ellis a copy of the poem – 'The Team In My Head'.
More Birmingham poems can be found in one of his books, 'Running Out' (Five Seasons Press, 2006) and the other poems there include those from when I he working as a poet in the NHS Mental Health Trust and at Heartlands Hospital. His latest booklet is from the newish West Midlands 'Nine Arches Press', a poem with photos of the demolition of the Titanic Café in Selly Oak.

http://davidhartbirminghampoet.blogspot.com/

This Beautiful Game
By David Hart

On the train back into the city
Someone tells a joke
About an old man in the stand.
Beside him there's an empty seat
And someone has their eye on that seat
Which is better than the one they've got
So they go down and ask him about it.
The old man explains
'It's the wife's only she's passed away'
And the man who had his eye on the seat says,
'You don't have a son who wants to come
or a daughter?'
And the old man replies
'They're at the funeral'.
The match has been a bitter-sweet secret
Shared by more than 39,000 of us
It's the same week in week out
This absorbing fuss
Differently the same
This beautiful game.

© **David Hart.**
David Hart, Kings Heath, Birmingham.

Vintage Villa
By Andy Lockett

Vintage Claret and blue
An aristocracy of sorts
In the transitory world of football – Edwardian
Civic splendour in the shadow of Aston Old Hall
A stadium worthy of the name
Trophies adorned
The red brick edifice
But they gathered dust and cobwebs
Walker, Hardy, Barson, Waring
Names redolent of a bygone era
And fallow years followed.

Fifties failings
Sixties shortcomings
Still, there was always a Semi
To bring in the pennies
Uncle Joe went grey trying his best
Doog went bald of His own accord
Despite the World coming in '66
The Villa Lion was not prepared for Tommy Doc
And Deadly Doug

Then came ignominy in the Third
Imagine Her Majesty moving into a semi-detached?
But they rallied
Forty eight thousand plus fanatics
Rocking for a crunch match versus Bournemouth
That's support worthy of the name
So, the long road back began

Little, Gidman both capped for England
Graydon, Cumbes the cricketing keeper
Claret and Blue to the fore again
Two League Cup triumphs
Then a long-awaited title under Saunders
And led by Mortimer
The crowning glory followed

Aston Villa, Division 3
To European Champions in ten years
Hard to believe?
Then – and now
Ellis came back
And rolled on, and on

Not a lot to shout about since
Until the Yank and the Prof arrived
Now, Villa Park is renewed
That Trinity Road Facade no more
The Holte End all-seated
Those 'AV' lights long gone
Tradition swept aside
But the pride lives on.

© **Andy Lockett**
Andy Lockett, Tividale, West Midlands.

Con Martin – 'Mr. Versatility'
By Peter Goulding

Con Martin was born in Dublin
And was one of the special few
Who played for both the Republic
And for Northern Ireland too.
Ireland's first ever substitute in 1946
Deputising in a friendly match between the sticks
Mr. Versatility, a centre half by trade
He always gave his everything
Wherever he was played.
Centre half, or right half, right or left full back
He often played in goal as well
And not just for the 'craic'
Thirty caps he gained as Ireland's best position-filler
A role he had for eight years when he played for Aston Villa.

© **Peter Goulding**
Peter Goulding, Dublin, Eire.

The Flying Irishman – Peter McParland
By Emdad Rahman

Thoroughbred from Dundalk
All out to pop the bubble
Fought Sir Matt's Babes to foil
The century's first double
Remembering the '57 final
McParland away Scott free
With the most notorious challenge

In FA Cup history.
Bull charge on Ray Wood
Smacking the Red Devil's face
Walloped and cracked cheekbone
Then won the Cup with a brace.
Villa's seventh and last FA Cup
Starring Johnny Dixon and Stan Lynn
Seamus with a decade of service
Houghton's gift from George Martin.

International at just nineteen
Five Jules Rimet goals in total
Propelling the Northern Irish
To a World Cup Quarter final.
In the Golden Boot race
Only Pelé, Fontaine and Rahn
Their smoking boots hit the net
A few more times than Peter Pan.

© **Emdad Rahman 2011.**
Emdad Rahman, East London.

Last day Villains
By Emdad Rahman

No Monsieur Houllier
To greet Dalglish the magician
Gary Mac sensed easy prey
With Carroll, Maxi, Johnson's omission.
Albrighton's sumptuous assist
Downing with the crisp finish

Scenes of joy quite hard to resist
Reds too clumsy and boorish.
Suarez skins Kyle Walker
Brad Friedal agile and lithe
Amazing save from Raul
But Spurs still confirm fifth.

© **Emdad Rahman 2011.**
Emdad Rahman, East London.

And finally, although it's not a real poem, it rhymes and it's the new Villa anthem on the terraces.

The Bells Are Ringing For The Claret and Blue

The bells are ringing
For the claret and blue
The fans are singing
For the claret and blue
Everybody is knowing
To the Villa they're going
Where the Villa are showing
We're the best in the land
Best in the land.
We're congregating
For the claret and blue
The fans are waiting
For the claret and blue
And today we're gonna score a goal or two
Or three or more
At Villa Park
For the claret and blue.

Remembering The True Villa 'Legends'

The definition of 'legend' is 'a person or thing that inspires a story coming down from the past.' In literary terms, no one wants to write a book or a tale about the moderately mediocre, the above average, or even the very good. You want to save your stories for the very best of the best, and the same holds true in football.

Legends are not just 'good' players or managers. Legends are not even 'great' players or managers. Legends are in a class of their own. They represent the very best of the sport. They are the ones that people hold up as examples of what kind of player or manager that they want to be. They are the ones that people tell their children about when they are growing up. They are the ones that are studied and observed by potential players and managers. They are the ones everyone remembers. There are many 'great' players and managers but 'legends' are few and far between. Internationally one can talk about players like Pelé, Maradona, Puskás, Cruyff or Di Stefano being 'legends' of the modern game. Nationally, we may talk about Bobby Moore being the English football legend of all time. We also talk about the likes of George Best, Bobby Charlton and Kenny Dalglish in the same context.

People often talk about players being 'great' but the word 'legend' is the most overused word in the modern game and the term has now become trite and is even used as a catchphrase on TV. So, how does a player join this exclusive club? Is it the ability to turn a match with a flash of brilliance or the determination to win at all costs? Do legends take football to another level, producing moments of magic which people will never forget? Sometimes a footballer's greatness extends to his personality rather than his skill.

This feature is supposed to be informative, so before anyone gets upset because I have omitted someone, or because you are convinced that 'so-and-so' was better than the players who are featured here please keep in mind that these are not rankings of the greatest Villa players of all time. Nor is it even my opinion as to who are the best players at their respective positions. Rather, this feature looks at players who are generally considered to be Villa 'legends'.

In terms of our club, Aston Villa, I could have listed maybe 12 or 15 players who have been called truly great players but the ones I have featured are generally regarded by most as being the club's 'legends'.

☉

Dennis Mortimer holds aloft the First Division Championship trophy.

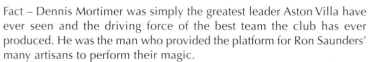

Dennis Mortimer

Date of birth: 5 April 1952
Villa League career: 1975–85
Goals: 36
Total Appearances: 406
Honours for Villa: League Cup 1977, League Championship 1981, European Cup 1982, European Super Cup 1983.

Fact – Dennis Mortimer was simply the greatest leader Aston Villa have ever seen and the driving force of the best team the club has ever produced. He was the man who provided the platform for Ron Saunders' many artisans to perform their magic.

He began his career with Coventry City but who would have predicted that his move to local rivals Villa, shortly before Christmas 1975 for a bargain £175,000, would ignite what would become a glorious career and the finest period the club have ever known in their history. Mortimer captained Villa to the League title in 1980–81, the European Cup in 1982 and the Super Cup in 1983. He was renowned for his driving runs and energy from midfield which allowed those around him to blossom and will forever be remembered as the man who lifted the biggest prize of all in Rotterdam on 26 May 1982 – the greatest night in the club's history.

Most memorable moments: how do you distinguish between winning the First Division title in 1981 and winning the European Cup the following year? Two astonishing achievements which may not be repeated by another Villa skipper again.

Charlie Aitken

Date of birth: 1 May 1942.
Villa League career: 1959–76
Total Appearances: 660
Goals: 16
Honours for Villa: League Cup-winners 1975, Third Division Championship 1972.

In the 17 years Aitken spent with Villa, the club's greatest servant sadly only won precisely one League Cup and one Third Division Championship medal. That sort of return is hardly what you would call value for such loyalty to one club. However, he went on to play 660 games for the club before moving to the North American Soccer League where he rubbed shoulders with Pelé, Franz Beckenbauer and Carlos Alberto with the New York Cosmos.

Aitken, was always an athletic and speedy full-back, spanned the great divide between Villa's 1957 FA Cup-winning side, in that he played in Johnny Dixon's final game (and also what turned out to be Gerry Hitchens' final game), and the mega-successful era of Ron Saunders but that in itself inevitably spelt the end of his career at Villa as he was given a free transfer at the end of the 1975–76 season.

Most memorable moment: 1 March 1975: Villa 1 Norwich City 0, winning the League Cup in front of almost 96,000 fans at Wembley.

Peter Withe

Date of birth:	30 August 1951
Villa League career:	1980–85
Total Appearances:	233
Goals:	92
Honours for Villa:	First Division Championship 1981, European Cup 1982, European Super Cup 1983.

Peter Withe will always be remembered as the scorer of Villa's most important goal in the club's history in their most important match ever – the winner against Bayern Munich in the European Cup Final of 1982. However, he had a much bigger impact from the time Ron Saunders brought him to Villa on the eve of the 1980–81 season when he forked out £500,000 on the journeyman 29-year-old striker, the club's record signing at the time but a snip considering the service he gave them over the next five years.

Withe formed a deadly and almost telepathic partnership up front with young starlet Gary Shaw, and he netted 20 times in 36 games to finish joint-top scorer in the League with Tottenham Hotspurs' Steve Archibald in that first season as Villa went on to win the First Division title. After five years service, Withe joined Sheffield United in 1985.

Most memorable moment: without a doubt, scoring that winning goal in the 1982 European Cup Final in Rotterdam and will always be associated with those immortal words, 'It must be. It is. Peter Withe!'

Peter McParland

Date of birth:	25 April 1934.
Villa League career:	1952–62
Total Appearances:	341
Goals:	121
Honours for Villa:	FA Cup-winners 1957, Second Division Championship 1960, League Cup-winners 1961.

A picture of the 1959–60 Second Division champions in the dressing room celebrating promotion.

Undoubtedly, Peter McParland was one of Aston Villa's greatest post-war goalscoring wingers; however, he will forever be remembered as the man who got away with perhaps the most controversial challenge in FA Cup Final history when he shoulder charged Manchester United goalkeeper, Ray Wood and left him pole-axed with a broken cheekbone and effectively reduced United to 10 men for the rest of the Final.

He was spotted playing in the League of Ireland and was signed for a fee of £3,880. McParland went on to play for the club for 10 years, helping Villa win the FA Cup in 1957 when his two goals saw off Manchester United. In his day, he was a defender's nightmare as he weaved his magic on the left wing.

His best saw him crash 25 goals alongside Gerry Hitchens and Bobby Thomson in 1959–60 as Villa pipped Cardiff City to the Second Division title. McParland also helped the club lift the first ever League Cup in 1961, with a goal in the second leg of the 3-0 win over Rotherham United.

Most memorable moment: his two goals against Manchester United which won the 1957 FA Cup.

Tom 'Pongo' Waring

Date of birth: 12 October 1906
Villa League career: 1922–36
Total Appearances: 225
Goals: 167
Honours for Villa: None

'Pongo' Waring was probably Villa's most prolific goalscorer, with a goal ratio of three goals in every four games. In one record-breaking season (1930–31) he netted a remarkable 50 goals in a season (49 in the League alone), in a season that Villa scored an incredible 128 goals, a feat that will never be surpassed in an era where Villa strikers now struggle to get to 15 goals in a season.

Although most of us will not remember 'Pongo' Waring, let alone seen him play, he was apparently a great natural footballer, someone who had 'everything' and was one of the most dangerous centre-forwards of the era.

Most memorable moments: during the record-breaking season of 1931–32, Waring scored four goals in two back-to-back games, against Chelsea (away) and West Ham (home).

Gerry Hitchens

Date of birth: 8 October 1934
Villa League career: 1957–61
Total Appearances: 160
Goals: 96
Honours for Villa: Second Division Championship 1960

The year of 1957 was a good year for Aston Villa as they won the FA Cup and paid £22,500 to Cardiff City for Gerald Archibald Hitchens, a relatively unknown former miner from Cannock. Although a raw talent, Hitchens bagged 40 goals in just 100 games for Cardiff City when Eric Houghton persuaded the board to let him buy the player he had been pursuing for a couple of years.

He ended that first season with 11 goals in 22 appearances as Villa struggled to 14th in the First Division, level on points but below city rivals Birmingham City. However, Hitchens arrived on the scene during the next three seasons and proved that he was truly dynamite. He scored 18 goals in the 1958–59 season as Villa were relegated to the Second Division. The next season, Villa and Hitchens recovered as he smashed 25 goals as Villa bounced back as Champions. However, it was his incredible season of 1960–61 that earned him a move to Italian giants Inter Milan and a call up to the England team by scoring an amazing 42 goals in 56 appearances as Villa finished ninth and Hitchens led the team almost singlehandedly to a first League Cup Final by bagging 11 goals in the competition.

That proved to be his last season in Birmingham as the lure of the lire was too hard to turn down for the Villa board and with Internazionale offering a signing-on fee of around £12,500 as well as a wage more than five times what Villa were willing to pay, Hitchens was soon to be learning the Italian language very quickly. So, without doubt, Villa's greatest-ever number nine and probably Villa's first iconic footballer, with perhaps the exception of 'Pongo' Waring, became England's most successful export to Serie A.

Most memorable moment: unquestionably, it was on 14 November 1959, when Hitchens notched five goals in an 11–1 rout of Charlton at Villa Park. It was the first time Villa had reached double figures in a League game since August, 1925. The fact remains that Hitchens still holds the record goal ratio for any post-war Villa player.

Gordon Cowans

Date of birth:	27 October 1958
Villa League career:	Apprentice: July 1974. Professional: August 1976 to June 1985, then July 1988 to November 1991, then July 1993 to February 1994
Total Appearances:	414
Goals:	49
Honours for Villa:	League Cup 1977, First Division title 1981, European Cup 1982, European Super Cup 1983

Most players only play for a club once but Gordon Cowans had no fewer than three spells as a player alone and now is an integral part of the first team coaching set-up. You would have to search far and wide and even then not get close to a more popular figure in the club's long and glorious history.

Having made his debut in February 1976 as a 17-year-old substitute in the 2–1 defeat at Manchester City, it was the following season when Cowans made his mark, profiting from Alex Cropley's broken leg.

Cowans helped Villa to the 1977 League Cup and for the next six years was never far away from a winner's medal as he served up the majority of the midfield artistry for the strikers to shoot Villa to the First Division title, European Cup and Super Cup glory. Cowans' vision, allied to Des Bremner's running, Tony Morley's trickery and Dennis Mortimer's leadership, proved an unbeatable combination.

In 1979–80 he was voted PFA Young Player of the Year and went on to be an ever-present in four consecutive seasons between 1979 and 1983, finally winning his first England cap in 1983 against Wales. But tragedy struck as, at the very height of his powers, Cowans broke his leg during a pre-season tournament in Barcelona and missed the whole 1983–84 season. He regained fitness for the following season but after scoring just one goal, at home to Ipswich in February 1985, he was sold to the Italian Serie A club Bari by Graham Turner. He returned three years later when Graham Taylor was in charge and he found his old form, later winning a 10th England cap against Ireland under Taylor (who had been chosen by the FA to become England manager) and the fact remains that he was never on a losing England side.

In 1991 Ron Atkinson sold him to Blackburn for £200,000. He returned once again in 1993–94, making only 17 appearances, before moving to Derby County.

Most memorable moments: Cowans was an ever-present for four seasons between 1979 and 1983. He won the Young Player of the Year award in 1979–80, but apart from that magical night in Rotterdam his first goal for the club was against Derby County in a 4–0 win in March 1977, 13 months after his debut as a sub at Manchester City and that day will remain in his memory.

Brian Little

Date of birth: 25 November 1953
Villa League career: Apprentice: July 1969. Professional: June 1971–81
Total Appearances: 302
Goals: 82
Honours for Villa: FA Youth Cup-winner 1972, League Cup-winner 1974–75, League Cup-winner 1976–77.

The Villa renaissance in the 1970s was epitomised by no one more than Brian Little, a player whose natural ability has perhaps never been surpassed in modern times.

Little joined the club as an apprentice in 1969. He scored on his full debut in April 1972 as Villa hammered Torquay 5–1 at Villa Park on their way to the Third Division title. He was a former FA Youth Cup winner alongside John Gidman but he found goals hard to come by early in his Villa career; however, the 1974–75 season saw him truly make his mark, smashing 20 League goals and 4 in the two cups as Villa gained promotion behind Manchester United and won the League Cup at Wembley against Norwich City, who they had pipped for runners-up spot in the League.

Then the 1976–77 season saw him at the very height of his immense powers, helping the club gain another League Cup win, scoring two goals to sink Everton in that famous second replay of the Final after netting a hat-trick in the second replay of the semi-final against QPR. Little netted 26 goals that season in a powerful front combination with Andy Gray as Villa finished fourth under Ron Saunders.

Sadly, Little made just one England appearance, as a substitute against Wales at Wembley when the hosts conceded goals for the first time under Don Revie. He rescued a draw for Revie when he made the goal for fellow debutant, David Johnson, in the 84th minute to level the score at 2–2 but was never to play for his country again.

Little was forced to retire in 1980 at the age of 26 due to a knee injury. He rejoined Villa as manager in November 1994 and won the League Cup in 1996, resigning in February 1998 with his team still in Europe.

Most memorable moment: that evening on 13 April 1977 at Old Trafford, when Brian Little shone in the League Cup Final second replay to give Villa a 2–1 lead against Everton must be the highlight of a short but wonderful career.

After Mike Lyons equalised for The Toffees, Little steered home a 118th-minute extra-time goal to hand Villa the trophy and firmly established himself as a true Villa legend. However, Brian Little will always go down as an immense talent with natural ability but whose career was cruelly cut short through injury.

Johnny Dixon

Date of birth: 10 December 1923
Villa League career: 1944 then professional Jan 1946 to May 1961
Total Appearances: 430
Goals: 144
Honours for Villa: Captained Villa to the 1957 FA Cup Final, played four League games in 1960 Second Division title-winning team.

Johnny Dixon spent much of his time at Villa Park playing in a struggling side but he still managed to enjoy 17 wonderful years at the club he joined as a youngster. Born in County Durham, he came to Villa's attention in the summer of 1944 when he wrote asking for a trial and signed as a professional in January 1946.

For many years the inside-forward spot remained his own. However, it was not until after the War that Dixon came of age. He finished as top scorer in three successive seasons in 1950–51, 1951–52 and 1952–53 with 16, 28 and 14 goals. Villa narrowly avoided the drop in 1955–56 as Dixon again topped the scoring charts with 18 goals in 40 games.

He skippered Villa in the FA Cup Final against Manchester United at Wembley in May 1957 and was voted the supporters' Terrace Trophy winner in 1959 and in 1960 helped Villa win promotion to the First Division as champions, albeit playing in only four games.

His swan song came in the last match of the 1960–61 season when, fittingly, he scored the fourth goal of a 4–1 victory at home to Sheffield Wednesday in First Division in front of just over 26,000 fans. Making his Villa debut was a certain full-back by the name of Charlie Aitken and it also turned out to be Gerry Hitchens' last game for Villa. Johnny also continued to turn out for the Aston Villa Old Stars, into his 60s.

Most memorable moment: undoubtedly lifting the FA Cup at Wembley in 1957.

Andy Gray

Date of birth: 30 November 1955
Villa League career: 1975–79 and 1985–87
Total Appearances: 210
Goals: 78
Honours for Villa: League Cup-winner 1977.

Probably the successor to Gerry Hitchens as a football icon to Villa fans, few strikers have ever been as brave as the Scottish lionheart Andy Gray, who enjoyed two spells at Villa Park at opposite ends of an illustrious playing career. The 19-year-old headed south from Dundee United for £110,000 in October 1975, signed by Ron Saunders and quickly became an instant hit with the Villa faithful because of his all-action style.

Gray collected the Golden Boot in 1976–77 with his tally of 25 League goals which took Villa up to the heady heights of fourth in the First Division but a it was a 5–1 win on 15 December 1976 over champions Liverpool, who would go on to retain their title and lift the European Cup, that will long live in supporters' memories. Gray and John Deehan scored two goals apiece with Brian Little also getting on the scoresheet before half-time as the gracious Liverpool fans applauded Gray off the pitch for an exhilarating performance.

His 29 goals in all competitions during that season helped Villa lift the League Cup, earned him the PFA Young Player of the Year and PFA Players' Player of the Year awards – an historic double not repeated until the 2006–07 season. Incidentally, Ron Saunders had refused him permission to travel to the ceremony, insisting the journey might aggravate an injury he was carrying. However good he was in that season, those accolades were not enough to convince Scotland manager Ally MacLeod to select him for the 1978 World Cup squad.

After just over one more season and notching up another 26 goals' the striker moved to Wolverhampton Wanderers in September 1979 for a then-British record £1.5 million. However, after a successful spell at Everton he returned to Villa six years later and would eventually become managerial assistant to Ron Atkinson.

Most memorable moments: unquestionably the brace he scored against Liverpool on 15 December 1976 and the two superb hat-tricks against Ipswich and West Bromwich Albion were the highlights of an incredible 1976–77 season where he notched up 29 goals in total.

Paul McGrath (aka 'God')

Date of birth:	4 December 1959
Villa League career:	1989–96
Total Appearances:	323
Goals:	9
Honours for Villa:	League Cup-winner 1994 and 1996, PFA Player of the Year 1992–93.

Two League Cup winners' medals in 1994 and 1996, and two top-flight runners-up finishes in 1989–90 and 1992–93, hardly do the man the Villa fans affectionately call 'God' or 'My Lord' justice.

Paul 'God' McGrath playing against Wimbledon in 1991.

Paul McGrath spent seven years at Villa Park after he was sold by Manchester United in the summer of 1989 for £425,000, a piece of business that represented one of Alex Ferguson's gravest errors of judgement – and undoubtedly, Graham Taylor's finest signing. It is generally accepted there was no better post-war player seen by the masses that the one and only, Paul McGrath.

McGrath had dodgy knees and he was all-too-infrequently at the training ground. It was rumoured that he never trained and only turned up to play on a Saturday afternoon. But where Taylor, initially, Jozef Venglos,

179

Ron Atkinson, Brian Little and last, but certainly not least, long-time physio Jim Walker succeeded was in comforting McGrath, nurturing him and coaxing out the very best in him.

However, it is perhaps a shame that such a modern-day great was treated to a testimonial against Birmingham City but only attracted a miserly 12,014 fans to Villa Park in May 1995. Surely, had it been held today then the Villa Park stadium would be crammed to the rafters.

The Irish legend who earned 51 of his 83 caps while at the club and later moved to Derby County in October 1996 for £100,000 before a free transfer to Sheffield United and retirement in 1998.

Most memorable moment: on 27 March 1994 when McGrath defied a crippling shoulder injury, which required pain-killing injections, he helped Villa beat former club Manchester United at Wembley to lift the League Cup.

Billy Walker

Date of birth:	29 October 1897
Villa League career:	1919–1934
Total Appearances:	531
Goals:	244 (a club record)
Honours for Villa:	FA Cup winner 1920.

Most modern-day Villa fans probably haven't heard of him, but discussions about Villa's greatest-ever player tend to begin and end with the one and only Billy Walker. He joined the club in 1914 and spent his entire playing career at Villa Park. Walker was a skilful centre-forward and a player who had the rare talent of being able to shoot with both feet. He made 531 appearances, scoring 244 goals, and is the club's all-time leading goalscorer and also stands second on the list of highest appearances and was a member of the 1920 FA Cup-winning side.

After retirement Walker had a successful management career, leading both Sheffield Wednesday and Nottingham Forest to FA Cup success.

Most memorable moments: in August 1920, Walker scored four of the five goals which beat Arsenal 5–0 and scored another four of five as Villa beat Sheffield United in December 1929. He was the very first player to score a hat-trick of penalties in a game against Bradford City in 1921.

All Kitted Out

Interest in replica football shirts has never been higher, largely fuelled by the internet and Sky TV coverage of the Premier League. Collecting replica and match-worn shirts has become a serious business and fans can now even purchase a range of high-quality replicas of classic shirts. In this section, I have detailed briefly, some of the changes Villa have made to their strips, badges and colours during their history.

Villa's first colours were described as 'scarlet and royal blue stripes' (or hoops). The next season saw the players wearing black and white tops and in 1878 they purchased a set of black shirts emblazoned with the Scottish lion rampant. The following season jerseys replaced the original shirts and it appears that the lion motif was removed after problems with the laundry. However, for a game played on New Year's Day 1881, Villa wore navy and white hooped jerseys and there is evidence that these colours were apparently worn at least until April 1883.

There is evidence that Villa changed their colours in November 1886 to blue and chocolate vertical stripes but evidence is sketchy for this period. In 1887, the Villa adopted claret and blue for the first time, though the colours were very similar to the chocolate and blue of 1886. In the early 1890s halved shirts were usually worn but from time to time they used plain claret tops with contrasting light blue sleeves. In 1894, Villa adopted the iconic woollen jersey with a distinctive contrasting neck band as their regular first choice strip. Long after other professional clubs switched to wearing cotton shirts, Villa continued to wear the distinctive woollen jerseys, with subtle vertical ribbing.

1876.   *1930s.*   *1957 FA Cup Final.*

1961. *1971.* *1976.*

By 1924 a modified design was introduced with a high crew neck with two light blue bands, repeated at the cuffs. These jerseys were originally laced at the throat but the lacing was quickly discarded or lost in the laundry and the neckline became stretched, giving rise to a scruffy appearance, especially when the neckline flopped over on itself. The older, single hooped neckline re-emerged several times (but the high, double banded neck did not disappear until the end of the 1955–56 season).

With the introduction of the modern, 'Continental' strip made from cotton in 1956, the club crest appeared on their shirts for the first time during their historic FA Cup run, which ended with them winning the Cup for the seventh time. It featured the traditional Scottish lion rampant that had first appeared in 1878.

1981. *1982.* *1994.*

1996.

2000.

Before he was sacked prior to the end of their relegation season of 1969–70, Tommy Docherty introduced a radical new design of strip and a simplified crest. The innovative collars with 'V' inset became customary throughout the League; however, this unusual strip was dropped after Docherty's departure. With Ron Saunders at the helm and yet another new crest was introduced in 1973. In the early 1980s, Villa, among a few other clubs can be credited with creating the definitive shadow stripe.

With the inception of the Premier League in 1992, Villa players were wearing a striking strip inspired by the iconic hoop-neck jerseys first seen in 1890 and bearing a rather more traditional crest. In 2006, Chairman Randy Lerner decided to make sweeping changes behind the scenes, which included yet another redesigned crest, which appeared in 2007. A small white star represented Villa's European Cup win. Finally, in 2008 Villa broke new ground when they wore the logo of Acorns Children's Hospice on their shirts in place of the usual commercial sponsorship.

Thanks to www.historicalkits.co.uk the 11 most famous Villa home kits are shown. How many can you recall and which was your favourite?

Trinity Trivia

- Aston Villa have provided more England internationals than any other club – 71 to date. (This is also a national record).

- Villa have won 21 major honours in their history.

- The youngest first-team player was Jimmy Brown, 15 years 349 days.

- The oldest first-team player was Brad Friedel, 39 years 259 days.

- Charlie Aitken holds the appearance record – 657 first-team appearances between 1959 and 1976.

- The most goals scored in a season: Tom 'Pongo' Waring, 50 goals in 1930–31 season.

- Most capped player: Steve Staunton, 64 caps for the Republic of Ireland (while playing for Villa).

- Most capped England player: Gareth Southgate, 42 caps (while playing for Villa).

- The highest outgoing transfer fee is believed to be the reported £26 million fee paid by Manchester City for James Milner in 2010.

- The record incoming transfer fee paid by Aston Villa was £18 million (rising to £24 million) for Darren Bent from Sunderland in January 2011.

- The longest-serving manager of the club was George Ramsay – in charge of 1,327 games from August 1884 to 5 May 1926.

- Ramsay was also the most successful manager of the club – six League Championships and six FA Cups.

- The most League goals scored in a season was 128 in 42 matches in the 1930–31 First Division season (This is also a national record).

- Fewest League goals scored in a season: 36 goals in 42 matches in the 1969–70 Second Division season.

- Most League goals conceded in a season: 110 goals in 42 matches in the 1935–36 First Division season.

- Fewest League goals conceded in a season: 32 goals in 46 matches in the 1971–72 Third Division season.

- Most points in a season: two points for a win: 70 points (in 42 matches in the 1971–72 Third Division season.

- Most points in a season: three points for a win: 78 points (in 42 matches in the 1987–88 Second Division season.

- Fewest points in a season: two points for a win: 29 points (in 42 matches in the 1966–67 First Division season.

- Fewest points in a season: three points for a win: 36 points (in 42 matches in the 1986–87 First Division season.

- The first football match played by Aston Villa – Aston Villa 1 Aston Brook St Mary's 0 in March 1874.

- First League match: Wolverhampton Wanderers 1 Aston Villa 1 on 8 September 1888.

- The first match to be played at Villa Park was a friendly – Aston Villa 3 Blackburn Rovers 0 on 17 April 1897.

- First FA Cup match: Stafford Road Works 1 Aston Villa 1 on 13 December 1879.

- First League Cup match: Aston Villa 4 Huddersfield Town 1 on 12 October 1960.

- First European match: UEFA Cup. Royal Antwerp 4 Aston Villa 1 on 17 September 1975.

- Record Football League win: Aston Villa 12 Accrington Stanley 2 on 12 March 1892.

- Record Premier League win: Aston Villa 7 Wimbledon 1 on 11 February 1995.

- Record FA Cup win: Aston Villa 13 Wednesbury Old Athletic 0 on 3 October 1886.

- Record League Cup win: Aston Villa 8 Exeter City 1 on 9 October 1985.

- Record European win: Aston Villa 5 Valur Reykjavík 0 in the European Cup, 16 September 1981 and v Vitória de Guimarães in the UEFA Cup, 28 September 1983.

- Record League defeats, all while in First Division:

  Aston Villa 0 Blackburn Rovers 7, 19 October 1899.
  Aston Villa 0 Everton 7, 4 January 1890.
  West Bromwich Albion 7 Aston Villa 0, 19 October 1935.
  Aston Villa 0 Manchester United 7, 8 March 1950.
  Aston Villa 0 Manchester United 7, 24 October 1964.

- Record Premier League defeat: Chelsea 7 Aston Villa 1 on 27 March 2010.

- Record FA Cup defeat: Aston Villa 1 Blackburn Rovers 8 on 16 February 1889.

- Record League Cup defeat: Aston Villa 1 West Bromwich Albion 6 on 14 September 1966.

- Record European defeat: UEFA Cup. Royal Antwerp 4 Aston Villa 1 on 17 September 1975.

- The highest League attendance at Villa Park was 69,492 v Wolves on 27 December 1949.

- In the FA Cup the highest attendance at Villa Park was 76,588 v Derby County on 2 March 1946 (This is also a national record).

- The highest attendance at Villa Park as an all-seater stadium was 42,788 v Manchester United on 10 February 2010.

- Lowest attendance at Villa Park for a League game was 2,900 v Bradford City on 13 February 1915.

- Villa Park has hosted more FA Cup semi-finals than any other ground – 55 to date.

- Villa was the first top-flight club to appoint a foreign manager in Dr Jozef Vengloš in July 1990.

- The highest-ever FA Cup attendance was 121,919 played between Aston Villa v Sunderland at Crystal Palace on 19 April 1913.

- Aston Villa was the first British club to give up shirt sponsorship fee in order to promote a charity from 2008 to 2010.

- Aston Villa have scored more goals in the history of the FA Cup than any other League club – 817 to date,

- Aston Villa have won more ties (128) and scored more goals (434) than any other team in the history of the League Cup,

- Villa have played 85 times in all European competitions, winning 40 ties and scoring 121 goals.

- Only one player in the history of English football has been murdered – Tommy Ball who played for Aston Villa in the 1920s.

Photographic Acknowledgements

I would like to acknowledge the following people for contributing to this book by allowing me permission to use their photographs:

Peter Fox, Birmingham
Ian Robinson, Rugby
Doug O'Brien, Erdington, Birmingham
Martin Pritchard, Stourbridge, West Midlands
Simon Hayward, Tamworth, Staffordshire
Emil Weatherhead Breistein, Bergen, Norway
    (www.emilwb.com)
Danny Drewry, Sutton Coldfield, West Midlands
    (www.midlandsmemorabilia.com)
Marcus Hitchen, Holywell, Flintshire
Peter Stokes, Quinton, Birmingham
Jack Miller, Liverpool
Geoff Mulvey, Tamworth, Staffordshire
Gordon Brown, Sheldon, Birmingham
Ken Baldwin, Lichfield, Staffordshire
Kevin Pitt, Walsall, West Midlands
Roger Hatfield, Sutton Coldfield, West Midlands
Ray Shaw, Nottingham
Darren Cassin, Ward End, Birmingham